Hoffenberg

Physician and humanitarian

Professor Sir Raymond (Bill) Hoffenberg
1923–2007

Hoffenberg

Physician and humanitarian

L.R. Humphreys

ROYAL COLLEGE OF PHYSICIANS
2010

The Royal College of Physicians

The Royal College of Physicians is a registered charity that aims to ensure high quality of care for patients by promoting the highest standards of medical practice. It provides and sets standards in clinical practice and education and training, conducts assessments and examinations, quality assures external audit programmes, supports doctors in their practice of medicine, and advises the Government, the public and the profession on healthcare issues.

Citation for this document:

Humphreys, L.R. *Hoffenberg: physician and humanitarian.* London: Royal College of Physicians, 2010.

Copyright

Copyright © 2010 Royal College of Physicians of London

ISBN: 978-1-86016-366-1

Royal College of Physicians of London
11 St Andrews Place, London NW1 4LE
www.rcplondon.ac.uk

Registered Charity No. 210508

Typeset by Dan-set Graphics, Telford, Shropshire
Printed by The Lavenham Press Ltd, Sudbury, Suffolk

Contents

For Lyle

Preface

Two thousand people came to the airport at Cape Town to see Bill Hoffenberg leave South Africa. Medical students in white coats crowded the lawns whilst other students and university staff in academic gowns watched from the viewing galleries. A contingent of women from the Black Sash Movement – Hoffenberg's wife Margaret (née Rosenberg) had been an active member – joined the throng which was interspersed with police and security officers – and their dogs. The National Anthem, *Die Stem* resounded round the airport followed by the great civil rights song *We Shall Overcome*. This was 28 March 1968 – in the era of apartheid. As his aircraft flew north to England, Hoffenberg had no way of knowing that it would be 24 years until he could return and 26 years before Nelson Mandela would become President of a multiracial South Africa.

As chairman of the Defence and Aid Fund which provided the defence of those accused of political crimes, and as a supporter of the National Union of South African Students, Hoffenberg had openly and courageously demonstrated his opposition to apartheid. This resulted in the banning order that prohibited him from entering any educational establishment. Under the order he could not continue in any capacity in the medical school where he had built a distinguished career as a physician and teacher and where he was engaged in laboratory research – particularly in endocrinology. To continue his career he had no alternative but to leave his beloved South Africa, accompanied by his wife and young sons Peter and Derek. He accepted a research position in the National Institute of Medical Research in the UK and so began a new phase of his life in which his intellect, leadership qualities and energy took him to the heights of academe and to some of the highest offices in British medicine. He was appointed William Withering Professor of Medicine at Birmingham University in 1972, and elected President of the Royal College of Physicians in 1983 and of Wolfson College in 1985 – for a time holding the two presidencies simultaneously. His prodigious organisational talents were well known and he was in great demand to head many other august organisations including those in the fields of cancer, heart disease and mental health.

At Birmingham, where he set up a distinguished endocrine unit, he gave priority to preserving excellence in clinical work and also to expanding the teaching role of consultants in regional hospitals; the importance of high quality teaching was something he was passionate about. With his colleagues he pioneered medical audit – a method for monitoring standards in medical practice. On becoming president of the Royal College of Physicians he further expanded both the concept of audit and its wider implementation. At the College he was also able to focus his attention on medical ethics – a topic which had long engaged his interest – setting up working parties whose recommendations continue to impact on many aspects of medical practice and research. His time at the College coincided with a particularly challenging period in relations between the Thatcher government and the medical profession; Hoffenberg and his colleagues in other colleges were forced to strongly defend the NHS in the face of the introduction of internal markets; he did not enjoy the best of relations with the prime minister.

His presidency of Wolfson – the largest residential postgraduate College in Oxford – also presented challenges which are recounted in this book. But he greatly enjoyed his years at Wolfson where his concern for the students and his firm leadership were greatly valued.

Hoffenberg was deeply concerned with end of life issues. In his early medical career in South Africa he had been asked to remove a still beating heart for transplant into the second of the surgeon Christian Barnard's patients. Much later he helped to formulate the criteria for (brainstem) death and urged wider public education so that more organs would be donated for transplant and more lives saved. He also strongly advocated assisted dying for the terminally ill: a view that put him at variance with many of his medical colleagues.

Hoffenberg was born in Port Elizabeth in 1923. He was both physically and intellectually exceptionally gifted – his broken nose was testament to his very active participation in sport – he boxed and played rugby and represented the University of Cape Town in golf, tennis and squash. He was officially underage when he enlisted for the South African army using a forged signature. He served in Egypt and Italy and although diligent in fulfilling his duties as a stretcher bearer never missed an opportunity for enjoyment – a characteristic that was much appreciated by his colleagues and friends in later years.

Throughout their married life, Bill and Margaret were known for their congenial and very generous hospitality which they extended to students, staff and friends alike.

This book charts Hoffenberg's life and career from his earliest days in South Africa to the final years in Australia where he joined his two sons and grandchildren and where he was appointed to the Chair of Medical Ethics at the University of Queensland. Margaret died in 2005. Bill returned to Oxford where he died in 2007 shortly after marrying his second wife Madeleine Douglas.

Hoffenberg's zest for living made him a great companion. He excelled as a physician, scientist, academic and humanitarian.

Brisbane 2009   L.R. Humphreys

Acknowledgements

I am indebted to the Wolfson Foundation, London, and Lord Leonard Wolfson, for financial support.

I am especially grateful to Sir Raymond (Bill) Hoffenberg for access to his papers, for many (28) discussions about his life and work, and for his friendship. The biography was undertaken on the understanding that it would not be published until after his death, so that he and his colleagues might speak quite freely.

I greatly appreciate my wife Lyle's editorial help and Jane Gilpin's care in typing the manuscript. I am grateful for Diana Beaven's meticulous editing and for Professor Robert Allan's support. Special input was made by my daughter Dr Sal Humphreys, the late Professor Robert Mahler, Dr John Penney, Dr Martin Francis and Dr C.E. Vaughan. The following institutions were of assistance: British Library, London; Open University, Milton Keynes; Royal College of Physicians, London; University of Birmingham Special Collections; University of Queensland Library; Wolfson College, Oxford.

I am grateful for the direct input concerning the life and character of Hoffenberg by: Dr N.J. Allen, Dr Mary Armitage, Sir John Batten, Elizabeth Black, Dr G.R. Booker, Sir Christopher Booth, Professor W. Brus, Dr Brian Buck, Professor Colleen Cartwright, Ann Cowell, Professor Bryan Emmerson, Sir Anthony Epstein, Dr M.J.O. Francis, Professor Jayne Franklyn, Philippa Franks, Dr Geoffrey Garton, Sue Hales, Dr R.L. Hall, Ayesha and Derek Hoffenberg, Peter Hoffenberg, Lady Madeleine Hoffenberg, the late Lady Margaret Hoffenberg, Professor P.J. Kanowski, Professor W.J. Kennedy, Professor Harold Lambert, Professor John Ledingham, Professor Maurice Lessof, Bernard Lloyd, Dr Mark E. Loane, Professor Robert F. Mahler, Dr Alison McDonald, the late Professor Ian McDonald, Dr W.S. McKerrow, Professor Fergus Miller, Dr Mal Parker, Dr J.H.W. Penney, Dr David Ramsden, Sir Gareth Roberts, Julian Roberts, Professor Michael Sheppard, Dr Basil Shepstone, Professor J.H. Stallworthy, Michael Tibbs, Dame Margaret Turner-Warwick, Professor Owen Wade, C.H. Walton, Lord Leonard Wolfson, Dr S.J. Woodell, Dr D.G. Wyatt.

ACKNOWLEDGEMENTS

I appreciate the assistance of: Dr V.S. Butt, Dr Andrew Day, Alan Gordon, Dr Victoria Harrison, Professor Catherine Humphreys, Professor R.L. Ison, M.A. Lehmann, Dr Dirk Moses, Janet Ottaviano, Professor John Pearn, Jane Potter, Professor Martin Stuart-Fox, Dr C.E. Vaughan, Professor Geza Vermes, Dr Peter Watkins and Dr Bryan Watson Brown.

L.R Humphreys

CHAPTER ONE

Port Elizabeth

Childhood

Port Elizabeth, where Raymond Hoffenberg was born, is a town on the southern coast of South Africa in the Eastern Cape Province. The sea surrounds it on three sides so that its otherwise balmy Mediterranean climate is windy. The nearby beaches and sand dunes figured strongly in Hoffenberg's memories of childhood.

In 1820 there was a significant migration of English settlers who built a chain of forts along the Eastern Cape Province to enhance their security. In 1995, Archbishop Desmond Tutu, as Chair of the Truth and Reconciliation Commission, chose to hold its first meetings in the Province, since 'this is where whites and indigenous people first waged full scale wars as they competed for the same geographical space'. Port Elizabeth became a successful settlement, its shipping ranking next in importance after the ports of Cape Town and Durban. Raymond Hoffenberg was born on 6 March 1923 when the white population was about 30,000. The extent of the black population impinged little on his family's consciousness at that time. As a provincial centre Port Elizabeth's commerce serviced the farming hinterland and provided a focus of education, law and administration. In later years secondary industry grew and automotive manufacturing flourished, transforming the character of the town's former more halcyon days.[1]

Dora and Ben Hoffenberg had four children, of whom Raymond was the third. Sylvia, the oldest, was five years older than Raymond, and Elaine, to whom he was closest, was only a year his senior. When Elaine was four she developed an imaginative attachment to one, Billy Ryan, who attended the Marist Brothers School which located through the Hoffenberg back fence. It is doubtful if she had ever actually spoken to Billy Ryan, but to assuage this deprivation she began to call her brother Raymond 'Billy', thus introducing a life-long confusion of names in which Raymond was known to everyone as 'Bill'. He was never so close to his younger brother Leon, who eventually took over his father's business.

Ben Hoffenberg was born of Jewish parents in Germany, whilst Dora, née Kaplan, moved as a young child from London, where she was born, to Cape Town. They were married in 1917 and first lived at Port Elizabeth in a small house in Rose Street. Raymond's earliest memory, aged three, was of the family move to a double-storey house, 'Brema', in the military reserve near Fort Fredrick. It had five large bedrooms and a very spacious drawing room, suitable for entertaining on a substantial scale. Raymond often slept on an open verandah, which he enjoyed and which in that era was considered healthy. Dora was the eldest of eleven children. As her mother died when young she helped to bring up her siblings who often stayed at Brema. Raymond later wrote:

> The youngest of them was Max, only about eight years older than me. He was my hero, a good rugger player, strong, funny – we shared a room for ages when I was young. [We never spoke again after I got into political trouble. He was a close friend of senior police and army officers during apartheid days and used to bring me messages to say they were after me] ... Mostly after dinner at night we entertained ourselves: two aunts played the piano at professional standard ... my mother used to sing well and play the piano badly.

His elder sister Sylvia became an accomplished violinist.

The Hoffenbergs' house had a tennis court where Raymond when alone would assiduously hit a tennis ball against the wall. There were many family outings to nearby beaches and to Port Alfred; at Pollock Beach he body surfed and in doing so removed a good deal of skin from his chest. There were also camping and fishing expeditions.

Port Elizabeth had a cinema but few other amenities. His memoirs recall:

> I remember the first traffic light erected in the Main Street (still to this day called a robot); cars used to drive up and down the street simply for the novelty of having to stop when the light turned red. I also remember the silent movies and the first 'talkie' to hit the town. There was a bio-café (cinemas were and still are called bioscopes in South Africa); it used to cost eight pence and you ordered tea and biscuits or ice-cream which was passed along to you from the aisle ... The clatter of cups and saucers didn't matter as the movie was silent and you read the subscript. Before the picture and during the interval someone would play the organ (a Wurlitzer), which rose up from the front of the cinema with the musician already in place, playing while it came up.

The young Hoffenberg's schooling started at a nearby convent for girls, went on to a Miss Duncan's kindergarten, and thence in 1928 to the Grey Preparatory School on the Donkin Reserve overlooking the sea. He passed through standards one to four in two years, remaining top of the class, and 'not very popular because I was regarded as a swot and was rather fat'. The junior school moved next to the senior school of Grey in Mill Park to which Raymond, having topped the examination for all Port Elizabeth schools, won a scholarship.

Bill, a schoolboy in 1933.

Dora Hoffenberg had a gentle, loving nature, but Raymond had a fraught relationship with his father. Ben Hoffenberg, having worked for ten years trading skins and hides in Southern Rhodesia (now Zimbabwe), had set up as a produce merchant in Port Elizabeth:

> Ben had a patchy business career: he made and lost fortunes, was a great gambler, and an international standard bridge player. At various times he invested in a cinema, property, a farm (pigs), a salt mine, a tannery, a hotel (The Elizabeth), wool, hides and skins. He died aged 76 in his sleep, having worked a full day before. He was charming and popular, a bit of a rough diamond, and lived well even when things were not all that good. He was widely known as 'Hoffy'.

Raymond feared his father, who in all his life never hugged him, but who beat him regularly for his frequent misdemeanours and locked him in the cellar as further punishment. In later life he said that only once did he have a real conversation with his father and that occurred shortly before his death in 1963. A somewhat wild child, Raymond became notorious throughout the Port Elizabeth district for his free-wheeling escapades; 'years later when I used to go back people would say to me that they couldn't believe I was the same person'. Sometimes he was denied family excursions, or sent to Grahamstown to stay with his maternal grandfather, Simon Kaplan, a fierce and threatening character. As a widower Kaplan felt obliged to marry his housekeeper, 'Aunt Tilly', because the mores of those days demanded marriage if a woman lived in the same house unchaperoned.

3

Raymond's childish, attention-seeking bad behaviour contrasts with his considerable moral rectitude in later life, but his lack of unqualified respect for authority remained an established character trait.

Adolescence

Raymond grew out of his delinquent phase when aged about eleven. This was probably associated with his success in sport, and the friendships this generated. When aged fifteen, a strongly built adolescent weighing all of 93 kilograms, he played rugby for the Grey High School first XV. He also became junior tennis champion of the Eastern Cape Province, played first class league water-polo from the age of fourteen and put the shot for the school. However, since he was younger than his peers he was bullied. To solve this problem he took up boxing at which he was so successful that no one else dared to enter when he put his name down for the school boxing championship. The teachers at Grey were 'all male and mostly ex-servicemen from World War I, some were quite unstable'. They used the cane liberally, and after one excessive beating of six strokes, each of which drew blood, his father took the young Raymond to the doctor, and secured a severe reprimand for the gym master in question.

Ben and Dora Hoffenberg on board the *Queen Mary*, 1950.

Sometimes a family visit to Simon Kaplan at Grahamstown was made by car, a distance of about 140 kilometres:

> The roads were not tarred and we kept on getting punctures. We had a driver and our car had two spare wheels, one on either side next to 'the running board'. Despite this we always had to take a puncture kit, a basin and spare water to repair the third and subsequent punctures. The car had to be started using a crank ... We also had to carry spare petrol as garages were few and far between. All along the road there were gates, each with a small native hut next to it, occupied by a family that existed on whatever was given to them as a tip for opening the gate.
>
> Now Grandfather Kaplan ran the town's tobacconist shop, a very formal establishment in those days – local dignitaries used to come in and choose their pipes and pipe tobacco. He also sold chewing tobacco, which was rolled up like a hose-pipe and sold by the foot ... Packets of tobacco swept up from the floor were known as 'gate openers'.

Port Elizabeth was predominantly English-speaking, but during the Depression indigent Afrikaans small-holders would come to town begging. Raymond and his sister Elaine would make sandwiches for them.

At the Grey High School Raymond won many academic prizes and medals. After early matriculation he was considered too young to go to university so in his post-matriculation year he took higher mathematics, an exam in Afrikaans (*taalbond*), learnt Greek and gained a certificate in 'commercial arithmetic'. During his school years, the most significant influence on him had been his English master, David Miller, who listed five to six books to read each week. They would discuss these, and sometimes he was asked to produce a written review. Hoffenberg's fluid writing style owed much to David Miller.[2]

Early in 1939 the young Raymond Hoffenberg left the constraints of the family home and Port Elizabeth's provincial milieu for the new challenges of medical science and the greater sophistication of the University of Cape Town.

CHAPTER TWO

A lance corporal in North Africa and Italy

Medical student

The University of Cape Town is set on rising ground below the great mass of Table Mountain where the white of the buildings contrasts with the green landscape. In 1939 it regarded itself as the premier English language university of South Africa and its medical school was highly regarded internationally. The precocious Hoffenberg, not quite sixteen years old when he entered first year medicine, experienced the usual euphoria at his release from home and family. He enjoyed the basic sciences of the pre-clinical years: chemistry, physics, zoology and botany. Whilst the teaching of functional aspects of anatomy received less emphasis than in later decades, voluminous detail had to be committed to memory.

Hoffenberg continued to enjoy sport – excelling at tennis, squash and rugby – together with serious beer drinking and a convivial student social life. He was nevertheless usually in the top two or three students of his year, and his companions were bemused by this academic success since he never seemed to let his social and sporting activities interfere with study. In fact Hoffenberg woke early, and despite the occasional hangover, studied in the early mornings, a practice it was his conceit to conceal. Alexander Walt was his closest friend; they subsequently stayed together through the army years and their postwar medical studies. From Port Elizabeth Billy Mangold, another close friend, was later killed in the war, whilst Stephen Connell and Tony Russell both died in aircraft crashes; the latter's death witnessed by his mother as he dived into the sea. These losses would help to sever Hoffenberg from his Port Elizabeth associations.

When he turned eighteen in March 1941 Allied fortunes in World War II were at a low ebb. Hoffenberg attempted to enlist, but his father urged him to complete his medical training. However, at the end of 1941, having completed three years of his course, he told the Army that if they refused his enlistment he would do no further academic work. He then sought to join the cavalry and was grudgingly accepted as a stretcher-bearer, where as a paramedic his training would have some utility. He volunteered for overseas service; since he was a minor this needed a parental

An undergraduate, aged 17, at Cape Town University, 1940.

signature, which Hoffenberg cheerfully forged. His training corp was based at Zonderwater, outside Pretoria.

Army training

Basic army training involved a great deal of parade ground drill, route marches and guard duty as well as the usual handling of rifles and machine guns. Exercise and 'physical training' figured prominently, as did handball, rugby and cricket, but Hoffenberg's recollection of his four years' army service is dominated by a sense of the profound boredom of it all; even in Italy, to where he was later posted, periods of active warfare were interspersed with long periods of inactivity. The development of a mindless uniformity seemed to be a prime objective of the training and he found it difficult to take seriously the value of many army regulations, the rigid hierarchical and linear organization, with at times the requirement to salute inferiors.

Since many pro-Nazis lived in Pretoria there was little involvement with the social life there. Some soldiers had even been murdered and so, for safety, troops from this volunteer army only visited the town in groups. For Hoffenberg, the positive new aspect offered by army life was a broadening of his social horizons. He had led a largely privileged life and the university was a relatively sheltered environment; now as a private soldier thrust into communal living he was amongst men from all walks of life and the 'real' world. He enjoyed the new comradeship of the ranks.

Towards the end of 1942 his unit left Durban on the *Île de France*, a luxury liner converted to a troop ship. Hoffenberg recalled:

> A Durban socialite called Perla Siedle (referred to as 'the lady in white' because she always wore a white dress when she took up her singing post) used to be told in advance of the departure of a troop ship and she would stand at the end of the jetty with a megaphone and sing such cheering songs as 'Will ye nae come back again?' I puked from sea-sickness for the first time while I could still hear her and a few hours later was admitted to the ship's hospital with severe vomiting ... While I was there a young chap from Port Elizabeth, Michael Richardson-Burl, whom I knew quite well, was admitted with acute appendicitis. I was feeling better by then and the doctor who knew I was a medical student asked if I'd like to watch the operation ... Michael was lucky to come out of it alive! The surgeon ... spent ages trying to find the appendix, and finally had to lose face and hand over to his junior assistant who found it with ease. By this time the anaesthetist was praying at the end of the operating table and I was doubled up with laughter at the whole inept performance.

Hoffenberg refused to sleep in a hammock several decks below sea level where he feared a recurrence of sea-sickness. Instead he spread his blankets on a spot on the upper deck, and slept beneath the stars – as he had done at his home in Port Elizabeth. Upon arrival at Port Said, the unit was transferred to cattle trucks and after a long journey reached the training camp at Khatatba, between Cairo and Alexandria. Here the whole division was immediately struck by food poisoning and, before the location of the latrines was evident, most of the troops lay with cramps in the vast field of sand until dawn.[1]

Egypt

Following the main defeat of Field Marshal Rommel at the end of October 1942, the 1st South African Division was dissolved and the 6th South African Armoured Division (6SAAD), which included the Pretoria Regiment, was created in its place. In February 1943 the 40-year-old Lt. Colonel

A new recruit to the 1st South African Division, Cape Town, 1942. Bill, Alex Walt *(far right)* with friends Pat Tebutt *(left)* and Hank Schmidt.

Evered Poole, handsome and debonair, was promoted Major General in Command.[2] The Division underwent an extended training in tank warfare in the desert, before eventually embarking in April 1944 for Italy, a quite different terrain. At Khatatba they undertook manoeuvres and route marches and were lectured on aircraft recognition, venereal diseases and first aid. The evening meal was served in the late afternoon, 'lights out' was early, there was no radio, and as they had to carry a full pack there was little space for books. Hoffenberg greatly admired Piet Duvenage, the medical officer, who was formerly captain of rugby and of boxing at his university and who had taken nine and a half years to complete the medical course.

> In the desert he used to come to my tent with two pairs of boxing gloves and say 'Come, Bill, let's box' and we would step into the sand and box. The rest of the regiment thought we were mad, especially as he was a captain and I a private. Once, by accident, I hit him harder than I intended and knocked him down. He lay on the ground grinning and said 'Mooi skoot, Bill' (good blow,

With the 6th South African Armoured Division in Egypt, 1943. *(Left to right)* Alex Walt, Peter Lax, Ray Mossop, Bill and Seymour King.

Bill)! I had a lot of trouble with one of the sergeants who used to pick on me to do the worst jobs and generally made my life a misery. I persuaded Piet to get him to join the boxing class … and then to let me get at him. I hammered him – after this he left me alone! Brutal but effective!

Hot water was scarce in the desert camp, and when Hoffenberg got leave to visit Cairo he would first go to a soldiers' club and luxuriate in a hot bath while his clothes were cleaned. He would end up at Groppi's bar where fights would inevitably break out between the British and the Australians, or the New Zealanders and the South Africans: 'The trick was to go upstairs and sit on the balcony where one had a ringside view of the battle down below without being drawn into it.' One night an Israeli friend of Hoffenberg's father took him with two girls to a night club, which, as it was out of bounds to lower ranks, required him to borrow a civilian suit. When the military police came and started to check documents his heart sank, since wearing civilian clothes in Cairo was regarded as desertion. Fortunately they were only checking military people but after this incident he stayed in uniform.

Some months later, on a week's leave, Hoffenberg visited Palestine, 'again in cattle-trucks sleeping on the floor'. His father's friend drove him about the country and 'at the end of the stay took him to the railhead where the return train was waiting … he kissed me on both cheeks in front of hundreds of jeering soldiers who were leaning out of the train'.

Since South African men never kissed it took him a long time to live this down. On another leave he visited Alexandria, a cosmopolitan and sophisticated city where he rediscovered clean sheets and a proper bed, and chanced upon a basement bar with a whole shelf of Johnny Walker Black Label whisky. He was happy to remain a private, but was given a lance-corporal's stripe which he never wore. He recalled:

> I simply switched off and took whatever came my way. I actually learned a lot about people I would never have met in civilian life. I made it my business to learn the military code and discipline and knew exactly how far I could go without getting into trouble. I was arrested a few times for trivial things like not having had my hair cut short enough or being late on parade. I would be marched into the commanding officer without my cap and with no belt. 'Prisoner, quick march. Left, right, left, right, halt.' I conducted my own defence which I usually thought was pretty good, but the CO disagreed. I was given reprimands and returned to duty, on one occasion with a warning that my stripe would be removed 'if that would matter to you', said the CO.

Hoffenberg subsequently volunteered for the paratroops but was rejected.

Southern Italy

Hoffenberg was attached to the Pretoria Regiment, also known as 'Princess Alice's Own'. In April 1944 the regiment travelled in a liberty ship to Bari harbour which was full of bombed vessels. It was hot and Hoffenberg and a few others dived into the water – which by contrast was freezing – and a rope ladder had to be lowered so that they could return to the ship. They disembarked at Taranto on 20 April, where the local wine stained irreversibly Hoffenberg's enamel drinking mug deep red. They then headed north-west up the Italian peninsula through Matera.

Allied forces, having occupied Sicily, had landed at Anzio on 22 January 1944 but had met with strong German resistance. General Alexander launched a new offensive on 11 May south of Cassino.

> The intention was to destroy the right wing of the German Tenth Army, to drive what remains of it and the German Fourteenth Army north of Rome, and to pursue the enemy to the Rimini-Pisa line, inflicting the maximum losses on him in the process.[3]

Initially the 6SAAD was held in reserve to exploit the breakthrough, and when this occurred it passed below Monte Cassino and moved on Route 6 towards Valmontone. Operating for the first time as a complete division, the South Africans fought a most successful action ahead of the Canadians at Paliano, 56 kilometres south-east of Rome, dispersing the retreating German army. Hoffenberg's *modus operandi* was to take an armoured car

Bill *(left)* and Alex Walt, a future President of the American College of Surgeons, pictured towards the end of their army service in Italy, 1944.

with a co-driver, which accommodated two stretchers, and to travel with a string of eight to ten light Sherman tanks, which were spread out in open country, or in line on the road; his was usually the last or penultimate vehicle and there was also an armoured scout car for protection. In his paramedic role, transferring the casualties back to a Field Ambulance or Field Hospital, Hoffenberg had some horrifying experiences. He and his bearer colleagues found that a body on a stretcher was too heavy to carry when they were crawling close to the ground and so even when under fire, they had to walk erect.[4]

General Clark's US Fifth Army took Rome. On 5 June 1944 6SAAD were passed ahead of the French through the city to Route 3, and moved quickly to Civita Castellana, some 53 kilometres north. 'There were fierce engagements at Cellena, Bagnoregio, where they stormed the heavily defended village, Orvieto, where they routed the defenders from the fortress-like town, and Chiusi, where they encountered particularly stiff resistance.' As part of 13 Corps they moved west of the Tiber whilst 10 Corps kept east of the river. They met with 'stubborn opposition, impassible roads and heavy mist and rain'. The difficult terrain added to the vulnerability of the force as they worked their way through Mercatale and Arezzo. Hoffenberg had been trained to dig in at night so as to be able to sleep below the level of flying shrapnel; however, they found that pitching a small tent safely over a ditch worked badly when unexpected rain occurred.[5]

For considerable periods the 6SAAD spearheaded the advance. The light Sherman tanks fought a protracted battle at Impruneta, 10 kilometres south of Florence. Hoffenberg wrote:

> We were the first troops in the city [on 4 August]. Florence had been declared an open city but the Germans had destroyed all the bridges across the River Arno except for the famous Ponte Vecchio. To stop us getting across they had blasted the buildings on either side of the bridge leaving huge piles of rubble that no vehicle could traverse. So taking Florence proved a lot harder than we had hoped. The engineers had to put down pontoon bridges under heavy fire from the other side of the river. Eventually we got across and the Germans retreated.

The Division was then rested for a month. Hoffenberg camped near Siena in the grounds of Castello di Broglie which was owned by Barone di Ricasole. He had become reasonably fluent in Italian, and each morning he and two companions would go to the cellars to taste the excellent wines and choose what to buy for the company: 'Each day we would insist on re-tasting all the wines that had been put out on trestle tables before deciding what to buy.'

The 6SAAD was transferred from the Eighth Army to General Clark's US Fifth Army. The speed of the Allied advance was circumscribed by the withdrawal of troops to invade southern France which, in Field Marshal Harding's view, 'was the biggest strategic blunder of the war'. He believed if it had not occurred 'Vienna would have fallen to Allied rather than Russian arms'. The next objective was to breach the Gothic line, 'a chain of formidable mountain strongholds above Florence from the east coast of Italy to the west coast'. Their offensive commenced on 13 September, and was initially directed at the Il Giogo Pass and through to the upper valley of the Santerno River towards Imola, the 6SAAD guarding the left flank, thus bypassing the strong German defences at the Futa Pass on Route 65. The South Africans, after capturing Monte Catarelto, reached Castiglione dei Pepoli, about 45 kilometres south of Bologna, as the Germans gradually withdrew further north. There was a renewed offensive on 1 October 1944, and 'between 6 and 23 October, in freezing rain and howling wind, 6SAAD seized Monte Vigese', won, lost and regained Monte Stanco, Monte Pezza and Monte Salvaro. Winter conditions then reduced the level of fighting and enabled the German Army to strengthen its fortifications.[6] Hoffenberg's unit was holed up 'in a slightly bombed out building that gave us some protection but the nearest water could only be drawn from an outside tap that put us in full view of the Germans who used to take pot shots at us ... water was collected at night'.

Hoffenberg contracted hepatitis after a convivial Christmas, was flown to a hospital at Naples, and then to a convalescent hospital next to the Rome golf club. He and John Toole, an old friend from Port Elizabeth who also had hepatitis, found they could have the day off if they volunteered to chop wood for the hospital furnaces. So they did this for a couple of hours each day, starting at 5 am, played 18 holes of golf, and their zest for enjoyment led them into Rome for the evening.

Now Hoffenberg was a superior poker player. His good mathematical brain allowed him to calculate precisely the probabilities of most aspects of the game and, playing with emotional detachment, his facial expression gave nothing away. He also used the common ploy of always being caught bluffing early in a game, and then bluffed no more.

> The people I played with were all deep into the black market, selling army supplies, I suspect. They used to get paid in Italian money – huge banknotes that we used to call blankets. We received our pay in small Allied Military Government notes, so you could always tell who was dealing in the black market. Anyway, I always won and I used to stuff the big notes into a kit bag. There was nothing I could use it on and I couldn't send it home. Friends used to come and say they had a couple of days' leave and were short of cash. I would tell them to take what they needed from the bag.

However, this somewhat hedonistic lifestyle was to be cut short when his convalescence came to an end. John Toole had a further week of convalescence; when the doctor came to examine Hoffenberg he used his medical knowledge to wince convincingly at the right place so that he too was given a further week at the hospital – with more golf and further experience of the Roman nightspots.[7]

The struggle for Northern Italy

Hoffenberg returned to his unit in time for the Spring offensive of 1945. The Pretoria Regiment, part of the 11th South African Armoured Brigade commanded by Brigadier J.P.A. Furstenberg, operated on the left flank of the attack which commenced on 14 April, five days after the Eighth Army had moved forward across the Serio River in the eastern sector on the Adriatic side. The 6SAAD was in the van of the 11 Corps advance and Hoffenberg recalls: 'German rearguards fought hard on the Ponaro [south west of Bologna] and delays in bridging the river prevented the early crossing of 6SAAD, which was now directed on Felonica, on the Fifth Army's right flank, which was reached on 24 April – by which time the infantry were on the line of the Po River as far west as Revere.' The South Africans were directed north to Treviso 'to conduct mopping up operations'. Hoffenberg's unit moved on to Milan. He was sleeping rough in a city square when news came to him that the German armies had surrendered unconditionally on 3 May. He then enjoyed the splendid victory parade Major General Poole organized at the Monza racing track just north of Milan.[8]

The decision was taken to repatriate the 6SAAD as transport became available, but troops could volunteer for service in the Far East, and Hoffenberg entered the list. However, he was first moved north to Udine, to guard an allied airbase, and visited Trieste

> ...which had been taken by the New Zealanders. Everywhere we went in the town they recognized us as South Africans and challenged us to a rugby game in the streets. The locals thought we were mad, scrumming down, using a cap as a ball, and tearing to the goal line at the end of a street or square.

Twice during his service Hoffenberg played in the Division's first XV, drawn from 7,000 soldiers.

Hoffenberg's unit was sent to Turin, and travelling across the Po Valley he acquired a small abandoned Fiat Topolino which only required petrol to travel as part of the entourage: 'this minute car wedged between huge scammel tank transporters'. They dislodged the partisans from the royal palace at Turin, but having occupied the city the South Africans were not allowed into it as it was regarded as unsafe.

> A friend and I found a ladder in the palace garden and climbed over the wall and had a wonderful night out in the town, being entertained by the partisans as we were the first Allied soldiers they had seen … I enjoyed my time in Turin. I had my little car and I used to drive down to the river every morning and scull in a beautifully sleek boat for an hour or two. There wasn't anything to do apart from very occasional guard duty.

Eventually Hoffenberg was sent to Bari to await shipment to the Far East. The news of the Hiroshima bomb, dropped on 6 August, initially brought him a great sense of relief, believing that it signalled the end of the war, but subsequently he realized the full horror of the bombing and its grim legacy. Length of service determined the timing of return to South Africa, and so Hoffenberg was sent on to Algiers to guard another airstrip. This provided opportunities for a good deal of swimming in the Mediterranean and visits to the Casbah at night. Finally the unit had a slow flight home in a Lockheed Lightning. Formal demobilization was delayed until April 1946, but Hoffenberg was able to commence his medical course early that year, well cashed up with undrawn army pay.[9]

In his early years – from 16 to 25 years – many of the attributes, interests, and concerns were evident that would shape Hoffenberg's later life. His cynicism about army culture and his sometimes dissident behaviour sat alongside his deep love of country displayed in his determination to enlist; those Ministers who were later to banish him from South Africa had not demonstrated patriotism in this way. He became battle hardened, but as a stretcher bearer his humanity came to the fore; he was fortunate in that he was not required to fire a gun in anger. He showed considerable enterprise in pursuing the more enjoyable opportunities offered by life in the army away from the battlefield, and was generous and empathic in his dealings with his comrades. Hoffenberg's intellectual, social and physical gifts would provide the basis for his distinguished medical career and attainment of high office in later life.

CHAPTER THREE

A physician's focus on research

Medical undergraduate again

The University of Cape Town, as was the case in almost all Western universities, was swamped by increased enrolments in the immediate postwar period. There was a great dichotomy between the young under-graduates fresh from school, and the ex-service men and women of more mature age, bonded and scarred by service experience and often more strongly motivated to study. 'Temporary' prefabricated buildings were hastily erected and remain in place in the 21st century. High barbed wire surrounded the ex-service men's residence, which with black humour was designated 'Belsen', whilst the women's residence became 'Buchenwald' until gentler sensibilities prevailed. Hoffenberg studied intensively for the final three years of his medical course, which included wide clinical experience at the Groote Schuur Hospital; the intellectual stimulation this provided was in marked contrast to the boredom he experienced in army life.

As in earlier days, his academic work was allied to a serious commit-ment to social and sporting life. Hoffenberg captained the university ten-nis team, and also gained blues in golf and squash. Subsequently he became President of the University of Cape Town Golf Club. In the interim he played a species of social rugby:

> We formed an ex-service rugby club as most of us did not feel like taking it
> seriously again. The rules were simple – no training of any sort, even running
> for a bus was prohibited. The social rugby [union] was known as the 'fish and
> chips' league and the other teams were mostly ex-servicemen. We used to
> meet in the Café Royal in Cape Town on Saturday morning and discuss tac-
> tics over a few beers. Then we would practise our scrum formation in the mid-
> dle of the lounge before going off to play ... The smell of stale alcohol in the
> scrums was appalling.

At the end of his sixth undergraduate year Hoffenberg got the second place, and was awarded the first position with the Professor of Medicine. His friend Alexander Walt was his runner-up, and gained the top position

University of Cape Town. Table Mountain is on the left.

University of Cape Town 1ˢᵗ Tennis Team, 1946. *(Left to right) back row* David Townsend, Vic Moore, 'Popeye' Villeirs; *front row* Jamie de Villiers, Bill, Loffie Marais (Secretary), and George Stelzer.

with the Professor of Surgery; later Walt was to become President of the American College of Surgeons.

In these final three years of his medical studies his social activities revolved mainly around ex-army students. He recalled:

> I did meet a couple of old coloured friends in Cape Town who had passed as white during the war and had been in the same regiment. Neither would join me for a drink as they would not have been allowed to enter the same bar as me – after four years of living together!

House physician

Frank Forman, the Professor of Medicine at Groote Schuur in 1949, was a superb diagnostician to whom Hoffenberg claimed he owed a considerable debt for having observed the systematic sequence of procedures he followed in assessing patients. Slave driving young house physicians was then, and until recently remained, a feature of hospital organisation. Hoffenberg therefore learned to work very long hours and to manage on little sleep; he was in the wards at 7.15 am, usually worked until 10 or 12 pm, and was on call overnight. In those days house doctors were expected to undertake routine blood counts and urine tests themselves, and to write long reports on each patient which included a full medical history, a full examination report, the investigations arranged and the conclusions drawn. After six months Hoffenberg became a surgical house officer but this post provided him with fewer intellectual challenges and less contact with complex medical problems; instead it involved him in rather dull and routine assistance at operations.

In 1948, aged 25, Hoffenberg had met and fallen in love with the gifted and beautiful Margaret Rosenberg. Margaret was also studying at university and was his junior by two years. She came from Johannesburg, to which her grandfather had migrated from Austria; he had become wealthy having developed the iron and steel company Robor, which was eventually taken over by Barlow Rand. Margaret had been to Kingsmead School which modelled itself on the exclusive English girls' school Roedean; after matriculating she left to study social work. Bill and Margaret were married on 1 December 1949 in the Registry Office at Johannesburg. He recalled:

> We had a patchy start to our relationship [in 1948], largely because I was drinking so much and still enjoyed male company ... Most of our friends predicted the marriage would break up quickly. We lived together illegally in a small room in the single doctors' residence as I was still on call at night. One of the nursing sisters gave us a tiny dachshund puppy which we called Otto

and kept in a shoe-box in the room – also illegally. At the end of January 1950 I moved out and we rented a small house in Newlands.[1]

On their honeymoon they travelled through the Drakensbergs in Natal to Port St Johns, and stayed for ten days at Plettenberg Bay. Two vicissitudes threatened their early married life. While fishing from the rocks, Hoffenberg embedded two fish hooks in Margaret's scalp. The local doctor showed him how these are removed by pushing the hook through so that the barb can be severed; Margaret had a partly shaved head on her honeymoon. Again, Hoffenberg, unused to having a companion in the house, one night at Newlands woke to the sound of bare feet on the floor boards and imagined an intruder; he ruggedly tackled the figure bending over Margaret's side of the bed and brought her struggling to the floor: it was again a damaged Margaret.

Hoffenberg and his friend Alex Walt spent 1950 at the Department of Pathology and Bacteriology at Groote Schuur which routinely took four young doctors in training for a year. They worked under the supervision of the great virologist Professor van den Ende – known as 'Duck', the translation from Afrikaans. The wide experience they gained in this year was to prove invaluable in their later careers, particularly the training they received on the nature of disease. They learned to collect material for biochemical tests and to stain and examine slides – at first some of Hoffenberg's conclusions were adrift until it was recognized he was red/

Margaret Hoffenberg, 1950.

green colour blind. They also learned how to conduct autopsies with the help of an experienced mortuary attendant who silently indicated where to make cuts, and they rehearsed tutorials and so embarked on their teaching careers.[2]

London

At the end of 1950 the Hoffenbergs decided to go overseas. They arrived in London in the Spring of 1951 where the severe food rationing came as a shock after the abundance and diversity of food in Cape Town, and they found the English climate Spartan. However, such deprivations were more than compensated for by the culture on offer: the Royal Festival Hall on the South Bank of the Thames and the West End theatres became their second home. Hoffenberg recalled that they were particularly enchanted by Claire Bloom's Isobelle in Christopher Fry's adaptation of the Anouilh play *Ring Round the Moon*, and judged the performances of Vivien Leigh, Laurence Olivier and Orson Welles superb, even when viewed from the cheap seats in the gods. Another experience that gave them particular pleasure was being able to recognise the London streetscapes – and sounds – and the tiny fields and hedges of the Surrey countryside that they had first seen in English books and films in their childhood.

After a short holiday with Margaret in mainland Europe, Hoffenberg embarked on a postgraduate course in the Medical School of Hammersmith Hospital after which he was selected for a post with the endocrinologist Russell Fraser. He became registrar of the endocrine unit at the New End Hospital in Hampstead (later absorbed into the Royal Free Group), where he worked for 18 months with Raymond Greene, and studied for the Membership of the Royal College of Physicians (MRCP). The examination had a very high failure rate to ensure that only the very best candidates passed. At his first attempt Hoffenberg survived until the final *viva*, when he answered a question on the dosage for a particular prescription. His answer was in fact correct but the elderly examiner snorted loudly with disapprobation: this so distracted Hoffenberg during the rest of the *viva* that he failed it. He passed comfortably at his second attempt. At this time his salary was £49 per month and his bank account did not contain the £35 he needed to lodge for his MRCP diploma. He presented a cheque to the young office secretary, Iris Rawlings – who was to become a long-serving staff member of the Royal College of Physicians – and managed to persuade her to put off cashing the cheque for a few days, 'an early sign of her kindness and good judgement'. He then sought out Barclays Bank close to Trafalgar Square, where the College was then located, where he found the manager to be equally understanding.[3]

During these early years in Britain the Hoffenbergs explored the Cotswolds, North Wales, Devon and Cornwall. They bought a 20-year-old Ford Anglia from a garage owner on a time-payment plan. In 1953 they spent six weeks touring France, went on over the Alps to Rome, and thence to Lake Como where Hoffenberg in 1945, when serving in the army, had been charmed by a lakeside village called Dongo, where the Tedesco family ran a hotel. Señor Tedesco was equally hospitable in 1953 and the Hoffenbergs spent a week 'with lovely food and drink and swimming', and boating on the lake. 'When we came to leave they didn't want to take any payment', but Hoffenberg insisted. The Ford Anglia collapsed and died on their return to London in 1953; Hoffenberg made the last two payments to the garage owner and told him where he might collect the body. Late that year they returned to Cape Town.[4]

Male and female

Hoffenberg became Registrar at Somerset Hospital, which took black patients. The consultant, Arthur Landau, suffered a heart attack, and the inexperienced Hoffenberg was asked to act in his place for six months before moving to take up a research appointment at Groote Schuur. This led to a lectureship and then to a senior lectureship in medicine with Professor J.F. Brock as his mentor. Initially, the Hoffenbergs rented a small cottage on the upper slopes of Table Mountain, where Bill would walk his two dachshunds in the morning and collect mushrooms for breakfast. In 1955, with a simple transaction completed over a drink, they bought a house in Noreen Avenue.

By 1954 Hoffenberg was running the endocrine clinic at Groote Schuur Hospital, which he established jointly with W.P.U. Jackson who had trained in England at Cambridge. Another colleague was Boris Senior. They found that a steady stream of patients who had various problems of sexual dysfunction were being referred to them and thus began their specialist interest in people whose sexual differentiation was ambivalent or rudimentary – a condition described as the intersex. Hoffenberg and Jackson sought to find ways of making accurate diagnoses and to provide appropriate therapy which would help to develop the full potential and improve the quality of life for these patients. They also set out to investigate and gain understanding of the genetic and physiological bases of the variety of conditions they observed.[5,6,7]

The genetic basis of the intersex particularly intrigued Hoffenberg and Jackson. They postulated a general theory which would embrace the great diversity of physical manifestations they observed in the patients referred to them.[8,9]

In a 1959 paper in the *British Medical Journal* they described 27 cases of gonadal dysgenesis, the failure of gonads to develop ovaries or testes. In seeking to provide causation they proposed a speculative hypothesis of the varying occurrence of three closely connected genes situated on the same chromosome.[10]

Hoffenberg urged doctors to be very cautious in allocating gender to patients. One medical practitioner had considered a 14-year-old girl to be female and had surgically attempted to emphasize this. However the patient developed as a male and when, at age 27 years, was referred to Hoffenberg he could only recommend stilboestrol (a female hormone) to minimize the male orientation which by this time the patient had rejected. He wrote:

> It has been shown that children begin to show gender awareness at approximately 18 months of age. By 2.5 years a child has assimilated his role as a boy or as a girl so thoroughly that a change of sex should not be made lightly. It is therefore of prime importance to diagnose the type of ambisexual development early in life and to assign the child to that sex in which it will be least incapacitated.
>
> It is a mistake to assume that the child must be raised in the sex which corresponds to its gonads. For instance, the most extreme form of male pseudo-hermaphroditism is completely female in body build and external and internal genital development. It is patently ridiculous to rear such a patient as a male.[11]

Hoffenberg put together his research papers on gonadal dysgenesis to gain an MD from the University of Cape Town in 1957.

USA

Stephen Stackpole of the Carnegie Corporation visited Cape Town in 1956 and offered Hoffenberg a fellowship which would have covered his expenses for three months in the USA. Hoffenberg managed to secure, in addition, a Cecil John Adams Fellowship, which enabled him and Margaret to spend a full year in America. There he was able to deepen his scientific education and to learn new techniques which provided the foundation for his future research at Groote Schuur.

In the New York spring of 1957 he worked with the Hungarian, Daniel Laszlo, at the Montefiore Hospital in the Bronx; Hoffenberg's mathematical skills were tested by his work on compartment analysis to track the movement of radioactive calcium around the human body. At the Presbyterian Hospital at Columbia University his fellow researchers Sydney Werner, Joe Jailer and Kenneth Sterling enlivened many aspects of

MD graduation. Bill and Margaret at the University of Cape Town with friends
Eugene (far left) and Mrs Dowdle, 1957.

endocrinology and gave Hoffenberg the opportunity to learn new biochemical techniques, chromatography and the monitoring of radio-active
isotopes. The Hoffenbergs spent six months in New York where the
Werners, the Laszlos and other colleagues gave them the overwhelming
hospitality visiting scientists usually experience in the USA; they ate
Thanksgiving dinners at three locations. Margaret worked in a central
office in New York which placed charity volunteers in the jobs that suited
their talents.

Hoffenberg bought an elderly Plymouth sedan for $400 and set out to
discover the USA; 18,000 miles later he sold this car, which had not missed
a beat in six months, for $300. In their travels he and Margaret visited
Baltimore, went south to Augusta, Georgia and called at various research
institutes as they crossed the continent. At San Francisco Hoffenberg gave
his first paper at an international meeting when he presented the results of
his South African clinical research on sexual differentiation to the American
Endocrine Society. Needing further education in nuclear physics, he
enrolled for a month at Oak Ridge, Tennessee where he worked day and
night to acquire the new techniques which were at the cutting edge of
radioisotope studies. Meanwhile, after experiencing the very basic facilities
of the Alexandra Hotel in this small town, Margaret fled back to New York.

A visit to Connecticut to see Norman Cousins, editor of *The Saturday Review*, left Hoffenberg deeply affected. Cousins had gone to Hiroshima and had brought back to the USA some of the 'Hiroshima Maidens'. The sight at Sunday lunch of their badly scarred, deformed faces remained etched on Hoffenberg's memory and would later give impetus to his anti-nuclear campaigning.

During this year in America, he was exposed to a wide range of scientific activity; he admired the tough rigour of the work he encountered at Columbia, Harvard, Baltimore and Oak Ridge, but he sensed that in such a competitive *milieu* some scientists held back information on their most recent work. Many of the contacts he made became lifelong friends and helped to open the way for his future professional links in the USA.[12]

Upon his return to Groote Schuur, Brock's confidence in Hoffenberg grew, so that he was given many additional organisational responsibilities: these included the choice of lectures for courses, the allocation of students to tutors and the organisation of twice-yearly examinations. He also undertook ward teaching and clinical demonstrations to the 150 or so students in Fifth Year Medicine. Rather than delivering formal lectures, Hoffenberg preferred to teach clinical medicine at the bedside.

A friend, Eric Flegg, told the Hoffenbergs about some new land for housing that was being opened up. They bought a one hectare lot, 1 Exeter Avenue, at Bishop's Court which allowed extensive views across the Cape

The Hoffenbergs' home and garden at 1 Exeter Avenue, Bishops Court, at the foot of Table Mountain.

Flats and from where the Atlantic and Indian oceans could be seen. A single storey bungalow was designed for them by Medley Langley who cleverly ensured that every room had a marvellous view and there was plenty of space to accommodate guests. They moved in on 1 April 1960, coincidentally a day of great racial stress in Cape Town. Hoffenberg laid out the large garden, planting proteas and other indigenous shrubs, and a swimming pool was dug. They now had a spacious family home.

Margaret Hoffenberg was involved with many family adoption agencies in her professional career as a social worker. After nine years of childless marriage the Hoffenbergs decided to adopt two babies: Derek, born in 1959 and Peter, born in 1960. The adoptions were successful; both their sons speak warmly of their exceptional, very caring parents.[13]

Albert Schweitzer

Readers may not know the popular sway Albert Schweitzer exerted on the public mind in the 1940s and 1950s, when people all over the world were aware of his self-sacrificial life as a medical missionary in the jungle of equatorial Africa. Born in Alsace in 1875, Schweitzer became a distinguished organist and interpreter of Bach. He turned to philosophy and theology, writing in the pursuit of the historical Jesus, and in 1905 started to study medicine 'to pay back life for all its goodness'. Then in 1913 he established a hospital near Lambaréné in Gabon, where his residence until his death in 1965 was interrupted only by occasional concert giving trips to Europe and the USA to raise funds for his hospital. Margaret Hoffenberg's aunt Clara, a contributor to Lambaréné, arranged for Hoffenberg to visit the project in 1962. Later he wrote:

> Getting to Lambaréné was not easy … A flight to Brazzaville with Air France was followed by transfer to a small plane that hopped from village to village, picking up or off-loading people, live stock, produce, whatever needed to be moved from one place to another. The seats were removed or rearranged at each stop to accommodate the changing cargo. From the airport at Lambaréné we had a short bus ride to the river, then went by pirogue, paddled by some of the lepers to the landing stage at the hospital. It was unexpectedly beautiful with large tropical trees coming right down to the water's edge and picturesque groups of women washing clothes and themselves in the muddy river.

The hospital was organized as a series of huts, containing bunks for patients, and was full of smoke as families cooked for the patients inside; the sanitary arrangements were primitive. The compound had a large population of goats, dogs and other animals which reflected Schweitzer's respect for the sanctity of all life. 'Schweitzer was everywhere during the day supervising, directing, exhorting workmen. Nothing could be done without his consent.' Hoffenberg twice dined with Schweitzer, who spoke in German but said little, 'flanked by two senior and long-serving nurses'. Hoffenberg found the medical standards of the hospital quite backward; Schweitzer rarely permitted the use of antibiotics and sophisticated techniques of diagnosis were unavailable. A parallel might be drawn with Mother Teresa of Calcutta. At the leprosarium on the hill a visiting Korean doctor believed that perhaps half of the 500 patients had been wrongly diagnosed and had been 'incarcerated' away from their families and villages for years. Schweitzer had not trained any blacks to become technicians or nurses, whilst his superior, authoritarian stance precluded socializing with black people. Hoffenberg learnt from a World Health Organization officer that at Lambaréné little had been done to eradicate malaria, sleeping sickness, TB or venereal disease. Despite this dismal picture, Hoffenberg believed:

> This is not the way to judge Schweitzer or his work. He did not seek fortune, fame, international acclaim. He went to Africa as a simple and sincere act of faith, in the genuine belief that he owed something to the world to reciprocate for the many intellectual and musical advantages he had enjoyed. He came to provide inspiration to millions of people, many of whom changed their lives to follow his example of self-sacrifice, charity and philanthropy.

Towards the end of his visit Hoffenberg was approached by hospital staff to become Schweitzer's successor. He was touched by this invitation but concluded that he lacked the necessary high-mindedness to isolate his life in this way.[14]

Protein metabolism

At Groote Schuur, Hoffenberg moved away from research on intersex to continue his previous interest on thyroid malfunction, but for a time protein metabolism in *Kwashiorkor*, a common disease in African children caused by a low protein diet, became his major area of interest. Brock was undertaking clinical studies on the effects of different protein diets and the frequency of protein intake.

Hoffenberg's mission was to understand the mechanisms of protein depletion and to develop techniques for its early diagnosis before the more extreme clinical symptoms became manifest; protein subnutrition could occur before the level of serum albumin, the conventional index of measurement, became subnormal. In this commitment he had strong and continuing support from the International Atomic Energy Agency in Vienna; his name appears on more than 25 research papers on this topic.

One mechanism which conserved albumin was shown to be its reduced rate of destruction.[15]

Hoffenberg's last paper from South Africa was published in *Nature*, about one month before he was forced to leave the country. He and his colleagues had shown that separate mechanisms controlled albumin synthesis and breakdown:

> Reduction or withdrawal of dietary protein causes a reduction in the synthesis of albumin, presumably through a reduction in the availability of amino-acids. Catabolism [breakdown] continues at a normal rate, so that a gradual decrease in the concentration of plasma albumin and pool size occurs. At some critical level, reduction in catabolic rate occurs. This is probably an attempt to conserve the albumin pool in the face of impending depletion. If adequate dietary protein is now made available, synthesis rate increases abruptly. The concentration of plasma albumin and the size of the pool gradually increase until there is no need for a compensatory decrease of the catabolic rate and normal values are re-established.[16]

Hoffenberg's research on albumin gained him a PhD from the University of Cape Town in 1968. Later, at the Medical Research Council Laboratories at Mill Hill in England he continued in this field but in the UK mileu began to feel that this area of research was less relevant so turned to other topics.

Rickets

Among coloured children in the Cape Peninsula of South Africa rickets, a disease characterized by crippling bone deformities, is a common scourge; 50 per cent of infants coming to the outpatient department of the Red Cross War Memorial Hospital for Children showed the symptom of cranial softening, and 25 per cent had X-ray evidence of active rickets. The disease is associated with a deficiency of vitamin D, which can arise from insufficient sunlight or an inadequate diet, the latter being the more likely factor in sunny Cape Town. Hoffenberg and his colleague Frank Harris gained a research grant from the International Atomic Energy Agency in Vienna to study the action of vitamin D in calcium metabolism. Their research confirmed that in untreated rachitic children dietary calcium was not being absorbed. Treatment of vitamin D had dramatic and immediate effects. They suggested two mechanisms to be involved – one an action of the vitamin on intestinal absorption of calcium and another directly increasing mineralisation of bone.[17,18,19]

Whilst this research was in progress, Margaret Hoffenberg, through her Kupugani organization, which had been set up to provide cheap food to the poor, was providing nutritional advice to help mitigate the problem of rickets: egg yolk and fish oil were rich sources of vitamin D, and breast feeding was a partial answer to the disease in infants.

Focus on thyroid

The manifestations of diseases of the thyroid gland are many and are particularly prevalent in communities where there is iodine deficiency in the diet. They range from brain damage in infants born to iodine deficient mothers, to goitre and the many manifestations of overactivity and underactivity of the gland.

Some of Hoffenberg's best research concerned disorders of the thyroid gland and led to him specialising in endocrinology in his later research and clinical career. He had frequently encountered severe cases of thyroid underactivity (hypothyroidism) on his rounds at Groote Schuur hospital and in 1953 he with W.P.U. Jackson founded an endocrine clinic there. They had particular interests in the eye manifestations of thyroid disorders and of the factors that stimulated overactivity of the gland. They also worked on developing more sensitive methods of diagnosis by the use of radioisotope techniques which Hoffenberg had first studied in 1958 during his time in the USA. With the support of H.F. Brock, Hoffenberg established a radioisotope unit at Groote Schuur. On his sudden departure from South Africa in 1968 Basil Shepstone – who was later to become a Fellow of Wolfson College – had to take over this area of research at short notice. He commented that Hoffenberg was greatly venerated and when difficult circumstances arose, people usually asked: 'What would Bill have done here?'

Among those who collaborated with Hoffenberg at Groote Schuur were Bernard Pimstone and Elisabeth Black. Pimstone came to him as an MD student in the late 1950s. His keen sense of humour combined with a commanding intellect appealed to Hoffenberg and they remained great friends. Their work on the actions of thyroid stimulating hormones was supported in the laboratory by Elisabeth Black, a highly respected scientific technician who later worked with Hoffenberg in Birmingham and became joint author of many of his papers.

It was in the midst of work on the effects of overactivity of the thyroid on adipose tissue, on which he was collaborating with Pimstone and Aaron Vinik, that Hoffenberg had to leave South Africa in 1967.

Mill Hill and Northwick Park

Hoffenberg left South Africa in March 1968 and flew to London to take up the position of a senior scientist in the Division of Biophysics at the

National Institute of Medical Research, Mill Hill. He was also appointed consultant endocrinologist at New End Hospital, Hampstead where he had worked in 1951, taking over from Raymond Greene, brother of Graham Greene. In his memoirs Hoffenberg recalled:

> And so we came to London. Things were not easy for Mum....and both of you, easier for me as I could go off to work every day and absorb myself in it. You went to Mill Hill Preparatory School where there was bullying and an unpleasant atmosphere. Mum had to get down to really hard work, looking after both of you, the house, the cooking etc. all in a strange country, and without the servants we had all been brought up to expect. It was fairly miserable, especially as it was an awful summer with almost no sunny days. The contrast with Cape Town was very depressing. Things looked up greatly when we bought the Elizabethan Nettleden Lodge [at Hemel Hemstead] towards the end of 1968 – it was a lovely house with large grounds and a nice atmosphere. We changed your school to Beechwood [Park, Margate] and I think you both settled down very well [as weekly boarders] after that. So did we.[20]

Initially Hoffenberg's successful adaptation to British life was facilitated by his being able to continue research in the familiar areas of protein metabolism and thyroid function. His radioisotope studies shifted towards human blood sera and rat livers. In 1970 Hoffenberg transferred to the Clinical Research Centre where excellent laboratories and clinical research facilities were integrated within Northwick Park Hospital, a new NHS hospital at Harrow in north-west London. Hoffenberg led the Division of Clinical Investigation to which he recruited a group of talented young investigators to whom he gave great freedom and encouragement, and many went on to chairs of medicine. He also established the clinical endocrinology service for the new hospital. Hoffenberg was a key figure in the development and management of the hospital and research centre. All the while he continued to practise medicine to the highest standard; he eschewed private practice but discreetly cared for South Africans in exile, including members of the ANC.

The development of endocrinology as a discipline engaged Hoffenberg's interest and he was actively involved in the Endocrine Societies of South Africa, UK, USA, Europe, The International Society for Endocrinology and the Endocrine section of the Royal Society of Medicine of which he became president. He published more than 80 research papers on thyroid function which are broadly divided into those dealing with the processes of thyroid metabolism and those concerned with the diagnosis and treatment of thyroid diseases. The publications listed in the Notes to this chapter amply illustrate his significant contribution to this field.[21–42]

Speaking at the Royal Society of Medicine in 1978 he said:

It is the concept of a hormone as something synthesized, secreted, transported to and acting on a target cell that I wish to discuss...and we now know that what is synthesized by a cell is not necessarily, what is secreted by it; what is secreted by a cell is not necessarily what reaches the target; and what reaches the target is not necessarily what acts on it.

He concluded: 'In preparing this address I have often felt a sense of amazement at the ingenuity of it all.'

Perhaps the most important legacy of Hoffenberg's research into thyroid disease, beginning in South Africa and New End and continued at Birmingham, was the development of a test to determine the presence of thyroglobin in the blood stream as a marker of the presence or relapse of thyroid cancer.

This chapter has outlined Hoffenberg's development as a scientist and clinician and described the varied research agenda he pursued. Over the period from 1948 until 1983 he gained an international reputation for his medical research, receiving grants from prestigious international bodies and invitations to international meetings, and he development an extensive network of scientific contacts upon which he would build in later years. His research served only to strengthen his innate scepticism.

CHAPTER FOUR

Human rights in South Africa

The historical context

The extension of political and civil liberties was the primary objective of the Liberal Party in South Africa;[1] Hoffenberg joined it in 1953, the year of its inception. The victory of Dr D.F. Malan's National Party in 1948 marked a turning point in South Africa towards 'apartheid', or the segregation of races, and by 1953, when the Nationalists had been further consolidated in power, various programmes had been developed to separate the lives of 'Europeans' or white ethnic groups from 'non-Europeans'.

In 1910, four colonies – the Boer Republics of Transvaal and Orange Free State, and the predominantly English-speaking Natal and the Cape – became constituted as the Union of South Africa in which there was great ethnic diversity. Three million people in 1959 were designated European stock; of these about 40 per cent spoke English in their homes and some 57 per cent spoke Afrikaans. The Afrikaners lived mostly in the rural developments. The English predominated in the towns and cities, where the Jewish community of about 120,000 made significant contributions to professional, business and artistic activities. Of the nearly ten million black Africans, who could be considered as coming from eight main tribal and linguistic groups, about 60 per cent lived outside the Native Reserves. About 1.4 million people of mixed blood or from minor tribal groups were designated 'Coloured' and lived predominantly in Cape Province, and nearly half a million Asians (mostly of Indian descent) were mainly in Natal.[2] Thus the Europeans made up only 20 per cent of the total population.

Hoffenberg's friend, the writer and educationist Leo Marquard, suggested in 1960 an interesting contextual view:

> This union of four former colonial possessions has become itself a colonial power, with all the problems that face those European states that hold dominion over non-European people. This fact is obscured by the circumstances that possessions [with a non-white population] are traditionally overseas possessions [but] the children of those who conquered in South Africa live side by side with the conquered …

Today colonial policy means a system of government designed to train Africans for self-government so that, as soon as practicable, they will elect their own parliaments ... To the European whose home is in South Africa there is a world of difference between granting responsible government to an African territory and granting Africans a share in electing the South African parliament.[3]

The policy of apartheid which evolved, and was made explicit by Dr H.F. Verwoerd in 1959, was directed to restoring tribalism, to making the Reserves into National homes with some degree of independence, and to treating the Africans living in European areas as migrants, subject to restrictions of occupation, location and travel.[4] It should be recognized that during the forty or so years in which apartheid prevailed and dominated both the national and international consciousness of the nature of South Africa, other social and economic factors were working to advance industrialization, African urbanization and other outcomes.[5]

Abrogation of rights

Discrimination against the non-European was well entrenched before Dr Malan came to power in 1948 but was steadily increased thereafter. Some discrimination arose from long-standing convention or custom, or from administrative practices; other forms of discrimination were directly legislated to achieve particular economic, social or political purposes.[6]

The right to elect parliamentary representatives had existed in a very circumscribed form for non-Europeans. Some 50,000 Coloured persons were registered onto a Common Roll in Cape Province, but were deleted from the Roll by the 1951 Separate Representation of Voters Act. However, this Act had not been passed by the two-thirds majority required by the constitution, and was declared invalid by the Appellate Division of the Supreme Court. Eventually the Senate was enlarged to secure a two-thirds majority, and additional Afrikaner judges were appointed to the Court to avoid such future embarrassing incidents. The right to elect three white members to the House of Assembly and four white Senators as representatives of non-Europeans was lost by 1959. Thus 80 per cent of the South African population lacked an elected voice in Parliament, although representatives of the minority Progressive Party, such as Helen Suzman, often spoke on their behalf.[7]

Restrictions on mobility impinged most acutely on the life style of the non-Europeans, who were required to carry identification papers and needed permission to be in a particular locality; this 'pass law' was enforced in a Draconian way. In 1952 it led to about 164,000 arrests and convictions which increased each year thereafter by some hundreds of thousands. The Government wished to restrict movement of Blacks from Native Reserves, and to prevent non-Europeans from settling in areas restricted to white occupation. As new 'black spots' became proscribed in white areas, people lost their houses and were moved to pristine locations, often remote from their work, and with infertile soil; their previous right to own household property was eliminated.

An African's right to choose his occupation was circumscribed by the Government's attempts to reduce white unemployment; black participation, even in skilled building operations, became debarred. This situation was exacerbated by the selective nature of education for black people and by their lack of access to quality schools: the Bantu Education Act of 1953 removed black education from the normal provincial education departments, restricted support for continuing mission schools, and revised the curriculum towards local language and vocational training.[8]

To the poverty of educational resources available to the non-European child may be added the inequity of access to the social welfare system. Dietary deficiencies accounted for much ill-health, (as discussed in chapter 3). The segregation of hospitals and the poor quality of medical care led to high rates of infant mortality, especially in rural areas. Much of the Hoffenbergs' efforts were to be directed to the improvement of the health of the disadvantaged.

The rights to freedom of association and of expression were circumscribed by the Nationalist Government. Access to public facilities became increasingly segregated. Marriage between a European and a non-European (including a Coloured) became a crime under the Prohibition of Mixed Marriages Act, whilst under the 1950 Immorality Act sexual intercourse between ethnic groups attracted an increasing number of convictions and gave rise to much police investigation; a Presbyterian Minister driving an African church-worker home in his car was at considerable risk.[9] Social activity between groups became difficult as sport was segregated and as multiracial associations were banned; reports of banning often did not appear in a Press increasingly censored or carrying out self-censorship. Censorship of books also isolated South Africa from exposure to the free-flow of ideas from overseas. There was a determined effort to unify the nation with the mores of Afrikaner culture, and to increase Afrikaner participation in finance and commercial activities. Political dialogue between members of different ethnic groups was discouraged and organization of trade unions was increasingly subject to Government fiat.

Finally, equality under the law became more honoured in the breach; freedom from arbitrary arrest and the operation of due process in law were continually abrogated through pre-emptive administrative action. The lack of access of the accused to legal support, and the torture, in all its forms, of non-Europeans in custody, were to become Hoffenberg's special concern.

It is a curious local anomaly that in South Africa the terms 'radical' and 'leftist' usually referred not to socialist attitudes to societal and economic organization but rather to an antipathy to the separation of ethnic groups and a positive attitude to multiracial integration.[10]

Hoffenberg in the Liberal Party

Peter Brown, who was later to become National Chair of the South African Liberal Party, recruited Hoffenberg in 1953. They had met one Sunday morning in 1947, when Hoffenberg, then university squash champion, had a vigorous game against Brown. Thirsty, they strolled to Brown's car, where there was a case of beer in the boot; 'I knew then we would be compatible', recalled Hoffenberg.[11] Brown – a tall young man with curly blond hair and a strong face – came from a wealthy family who owned farms and a wholesale business in Natal; he was studying native law and administration in the same class as Margaret Rosenberg (later Hoffenberg). Hoffenberg sometimes stayed in Brown's fishing shack in the Drakensberg Mountains, where he first met Alan Paton, the author of the best-selling, seminal novel, *Cry The Beloved Country*. Paton, together with Leo Marquard, Oscar Wollheim and Margaret Ballinger, provided the main inspiration for the formation of the Liberal Association, which became the Liberal Party on 9 May 1953, after the re-election of the Nationalist Party. The Liberal Party emerged partly from disillusionment with the acceptance by the United Party of the racist policies of the Government, and enunciated the following principles:

1. The essential dignity of every human being irrespective of race, colour or creed, and the maintenance of his fundamental rights;
2. The right of every human being to develop to the fullest extent of which he is capable consistent with the rights of others;
3. The maintenance of the rule of law;
4. That no person be debarred from participating in the government and other democratic processes of the country by reason only of race, colour or creed, and that political rights based on a common franchise roll be extended to all suitably qualified persons.[12]

Janet Robertson reported that the party would employ 'only democratic and constitutional means' to implement their principles, and would oppose 'all forms of totalitarianism such as communism and fascism'. The possible deletion of the last five words was hotly debated in 1954, and within the Party there were always divisions of attitude to communism, although the majority of members, led by Alan Paton, were anti-communist. Initially membership was predominantly European, but by the 1960s non-Europeans formed the majority. The Party endorsed universal suffrage when Hoffenberg attended its National Congress in 1960 and gradually it began to campaign more assiduously on economic issues.[13]

Sharpville and after

The British Prime Minister, Harold Macmillan, stunned many South Africans and caught the world's attention with his prescient declaration in a speech to parliament in Cape Town in February 1960:

> The wind of change is blowing through this continent ... this growth of national consciousness is a political fact ... to create a society which respects the rights of individuals ... Individual merit, and individual merit alone, is the criterion for man's advancement, whether political or economic ... I hope you won't mind my saying frankly that there are some aspects of your policies which make it impossible for us to [support and encourage you] without being false to our own deep convictions about the political destinies of free men.[14]

Hoffenberg happened to hear this on his radio, and was bemused by the absence of a negative response by Verwoerd, who appeared not to have absorbed the gamut of the speech.

The Pan-Africanist Congress, a militant offshoot of the African National Congress, launched a campaign to abolish the pass laws. In support of this campaign on 21 March 1960 a large crowd assembled at Sharpville in the Transvaal; police opened fire and killed 67 Africans and wounded 186. At Langa near Cape Town there was also a large demonstration, with fewer casualties.[15]

Up to this point Hoffenberg had attended some Liberal Party meetings, but had been preoccupied mainly by his vocation in medical science. He and Margaret now thought deeply about their position, and decided to stay in South Africa and to commit themselves more fully to African advancement. Margaret was a member of the Black Sash Movement. Hoffenberg wrote:

> This was formed by a group of women initially to protest against a change in the Constitution that allowed the removal of Coloured people from the voters' roll. It grew into an important source of advice to black people about their (limited) legal rights ... They used to hold silent protests over increasingly restrictive laws and harsh practices, standing in complete silence at prominent sites in the cities, wearing white dresses with a black sash across their tops. Pro-apartheid thugs would confront them and hurl abuse, often racist and obscenely sexist, which they would endure without reacting. They would not allow any of us (males) to 'protect' them as they did not wish to risk violence.[16]

Actually Hoffenberg would sometimes park his car unobtrusively on a slight rise about 200 metres from the Anglican Cathedral to hold a watching brief over the vigil.

Whilst Hoffenberg worked to understand the mechanisms of the Kwashiorkor disease and to develop early diagnosis before the extreme clinical symptoms were manifest, Margaret attacked the problem of improving the availability of protein in the South African communities. Some 1,200 cases of Kwashiorkor were notified per month, and infant mortality was high. She started the Kupugani organization in the Western Cape in 1963. Kupugani, meaning 'uplift yourself' in Zulu, began in Natal when a Mrs Eileen Alcock developed a scheme for selling surplus milk at low prices to needy people. Margaret flung herself into the movement with great energy and by 1964 there were 200 branches and seven regional offices. Her organizational flair was directed to recruiting volunteers who would work in food distribution outlets and to the education of the community in the advantages of Kupugani foods – 'the thousands of tons of milk, fortified soups, biscuits, peanut butter and other foods that left the premises each month' – which were making an impact on improving the health of the disadvantaged. Kupugani negotiated low price contracts for bulk supplies and absorbed some seasonal surpluses of agricultural products through negotiations with bodies such as the Egg Board. They were thus able to sell to school children a tasty, nourishing soup for half a cent per bowl, and a nutritious meal for one cent. Margaret also persuaded some companies and firms to provide highly fortified protein foods to their workers and engaged a number of welfare agencies and churches in the programme.[17]

As a South African public servant Hoffenberg was supposed not to engage in political activity, although this rule was honoured in the breach by the many Afrikaners who were active in the Broederbond organization dedicated to furthering Afrikaner interests. Consequently, although he had joined the Liberal Party, he did not hold office, except in an informal capacity. The Institute of Race Relations and the Defence and Aid Fund were in a different category, since they were not political parties. In 1962 Hoffenberg wrote to the *British Medical Journal* expounding the need to improve medical education for non-whites. He referred to the great difficulty many students faced in funding their years in a medical course, and in coping with inadequate education prior to entry. At university these students were precluded from seeing white patients and were now excluded from the University of Witwatersrand by the Extension of Universities Education Act (*sic*). Upon graduation they were unable to supervise white nurses or doctors, were paid less than white doctors, and had fewer opportunities for postgraduate study. 'Segregated universities', Hoffenberg wrote, 'are yet another symbol of racial oppression and, as such, they are despised …'[18]

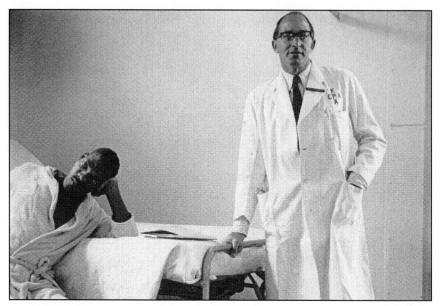

Attending a patient with acromegaly, a member of Pan African Congress, at Groote Schuur Hospital.

He continued this polemic when Dr T.E.W. Schumann, Deputy Chairman of the South African Atomic Energy Board, expressed outrage that the journal *Nature* should publish two editorials critical of apartheid in South African learned societies and claimed 'a high degree of moral discipline'. Hoffenberg's rejoinder drew a parallel with the situation in Germany 'when Nazi "scientists" strove to defend their racialistic principles against the censure of the civilized world'.[19]

In 1963 Hoffenberg mounted a campaign against solitary confinement, as practised under the Government's 90-day detention clause. He and Professor K. Danziger did not acknowledge their authorship of a petition signed by 60 leading psychiatrists, psychologists and medical specialists, which described solitary confinement as inhuman and unjustifiable, and as leading to intense distress and impairment of certain mental functions. The petition suggested that because of the mental deterioration of the detainee, the results of interrogation might be unreliable. The petition attracted considerable publicity but no subsequent softening of Government attitudes.[20]

Project support

On his overseas visits to scientific meetings Hoffenberg sought funds and publicity for his projects. He found particularly strong support in Britain.

Sometimes he was able to place case studies of abused prisoners in *The Observer* newspaper, without attribution, and he briefed the journalist and Conservative Minister, Iain Macleod, for a long article about the role of the Liberal Party in South African politics. He secured funding from Canon John Collins' group for the Defence and Aid Fund, which contracted lawyers in the defence of people accused of political crimes and misdemeanours. The Labour politician Barbara Castle was sympathetic to his causes. Barney Heyhoe, a Conservative Minister, ensured the Ariel Foundation helped to fund *Contact*, the South African Liberal Party newspaper, which was edited superbly in its early days by Patrick Duncan, son of the former Governor-General.

Subsequently Hoffenberg learnt that the Ariel Foundation was supported by the Congress of Cultural Freedom, which in turn was secretly funded by the U.S. Central Intelligence Agency (CIA). Hoffenberg's circle of friends included many diplomats and in later years an American friend confessed that he had been the CIA Station Chief in South Africa and had considered attempting to recruit Hoffenberg. However, when the latter spoke on the same platform as the left-wing Albie Sachs it was decided that he was too soft on communism. Later, at a dinner in London, when Hoffenberg introduced Sachs, then a judge of the South African Constitution Court, he was able to indicate how Sachs had rescued him from a potential career in the CIA.[21]

The College of Advanced Education and Training (CADET) was conceived by Leo Marquard, Hoffenberg, Ian Robertson and Jonty Driver of the National Union of South African Students (NUSAS), and others; they planned to advance black South African leadership in society with a one-year programme in English writing skills, economics and history. Patrick van Rensburg, a former Liberal Party organizer, had established a school in Bechuanaland (Botswana) and Sir Seretse Khama arranged a grant of land for the College, whilst Professor Julian Beinart designed the buildings. The UK Minister, Mrs Eirene White, supported the proposal but the South African Government was alarmed by the prospect of dissidents emerging from Bechuanaland and successfully pressured the UK Government to abort the project.

Margaret Hoffenberg was a generous hostess, and 1 Exeter Avenue became one of the intellectual centres of Cape Town where writers such as Leo Marquard would meet with leading black Africans, such as Hoffenberg's friend the Reverend Clive McBride. It was one of the few places where people of different races could meet. Journalists, politicians, artists and scientists, when visiting from overseas, found the Hoffenbergs provided a rare opportunity to interact with non-Europeans and to hear views alternative to the official Government line. Their house 'became a second home to many

Leo Marquard in the Hoffenbergs' garden at 1 Exeter Avenue.

students of liberal disposition, and hardly an evening or weekend passed without 6–10 people coming in for a drink, a meal or simply a chance to speak about how they felt'. Hoffenberg wrote: 'many of those students are like family to this day and we still keep in touch.' His young cousin, Andrea Durbach, wrote that 'he lived in a house at the top of the hill, filled with laughter ... and people who talked of politics and foreign lands'.[22]

The African Resistance Movement

Electoral success eluded the Liberal Party; in the October 1961 election they received 2,461 votes in the four constituencies they contested, in a total electorate of 800,590. Their major electoral achievement occurred in the November 1963 Transkei elections where vigorous campaigning led to the election of a majority of anti-government black candidates. The Party's economic policies sought to focus more on benefits to the non-white population and in May 1961 its declared objectives were 'to remove the industrial colour-bar, fix minimum wages, provide compulsory education, raise taxes on the rich and extend social welfare to all sections'. Hoffenberg was wholly anti-communist, had no interest in communism and never attended a Communist Party meeting, but at this time had some sympathy for the Liberal Party's endorsement of the need to nationalize some natural resources.[23]

Hoffenberg was committed to change through constitutional means and opposed to violence. One Sunday morning when Alan Paton was staying at his home they went to a beach near Cape Town. There they saw

Randolph Vigne and Eddie Daniels, and Adrian Leftwich of the National Union of South African Students (NUSAS) strolling on the sands. When these three sighted Hoffenberg and Paton they abruptly turned and went in the opposite direction; presumably they were speaking out of earshot of listening devices and acting conspiratorially. Vigne subsequently admitted to Hoffenberg that he was involved in the National Committee of Liberation, later called the African Resistance Movement (ARM). This organization arose from the coalition of five groups disillusioned with the rate of South Africa's progress towards democracy:

> They shared the conviction that since all lawful opposition was now banned, violence was the only way to continue the fight against white supremacy ... [but] they held a firm commitment that sabotage should not bring injury to people ... they tended to be deeply suspicious of the Communist Party.[24]

A former member of ARM, Magnus Gunther, has written a detailed account of the precepts, membership and operations of ARM. Diverse philosophies were held by the members, and Gunther suggests the consensus view was 'insurrectionary democratic socialism', signifying:

- A commitment to democracy sustained by rights of free speech, association, elections and press, due process of the law ... The violent assumption of power by a minority was unacceptable ...
- The indispensable State would remain an enduring basis for creating the conditions for equality and freedom.
- Nationalisation of the commanding heights of the economy [only] ...
- A view that class antagonism was [not] irreconcilable ...
- No reliance on an assured 'historical inevitability' of socialist development.[25]

They were reformists rather than revolutionaries. The tall and energetic Randolph Vigne, editor and publisher, became the doyen of ARM and Adrian Leftwich its chief organizer. A little over half of the 58 members of ARM which Gunther listed were also members of the Liberal Party. In this they transgressed the constitution of the Liberal Party, which eschewed sabotage; Vigne suggested resignation from the Liberal Party would have attracted Security attention. Some members were only interested in action and not in political philosophy.

The initial focus of ARM in 1961 was on assisting dissidents into exile from South Africa. They then embarked on a series of attacks on public property; electricity pylons were a favoured target and the subsequent blackouts attracted public notice. Although these attacks were carried out by amateurs, Gunther declared that the logistics were carefully planned, and the 25 acts of sabotage carried out over three years on a shoestring budget proved more effective than those undertaken by the black African MK organization at this time.[26]

Antiapartheid activists Jonty Driver *(left)*, Bill, and Patrick Van Rensburg *(right)* in Botswana, 1963.

The South African Government banned Randolph Vigne under the Suppression of Communism Act in March 1963 and in the ensuing 14 months a further nine Liberal Party leaders were banned. Alan Paton protested that it was absurd to link the Liberal Party to the bombings. This prompted Hoffenberg to fly to Natal, where in the remote Drakensbergs he counselled Alan Paton to avoid such statements, as he knew Liberal Party members were involved in ARM. Paton was appalled, since he had received direct assurances from the specific members that they were not involved.[27]

In July 1964 Hoffenberg happened to be in the Cape Town Liberal Party office when the phone rang and an unknown speaker said: 'Eddie Daniels has been arrested.' Hoffenberg strolled around to Randolph Vigne's office to pass on this news. Vigne turned white and left the building; with the help of friends he next surfaced in Canada. His wife Gillian rang Hoffenberg, whose telephone line was tapped. When she told him that Randolph was safely overseas, there was an exclamatory 'O God!!' from the listener; clearly this was disappointing news for Security. Gillian came to dinner at the Hoffenbergs before sailing to the UK. Hoffenberg had been treating her asthma, and as she left he carried out to her car a wooden box containing medicines for the voyage. It had been raining heavily and next morning Security raided Gillian's home and were no doubt disappointed to discover the box only contained tablets; Hoffenberg derived some satisfaction at the thought of those Security men standing all the evening to no purpose in the rain in the trees near his house.

On 24 July 1964, John Harris, a recent recruit to ARM, placed a bomb in a cubicle in the main concourse of Johannesburg Railway Station. He rang the police 13 minutes before the bomb exploded, but no action was taken to remove it or the people from the concourse. It killed an elderly white woman and injured another 23 people. Now Adrian Leftwich of the NUSAS had been taken into police custody. Hoffenberg said no one should be criticized for revealing names in these circumstances, but Leftwich not only became a State witness at the trial of Harris, who was executed, but gratuitously volunteered the names and also some identifying characteristics of other colleagues in hiding. As a result of this information, the young student Alan Brookes was identified and sentenced to prison. Subsequently Leftwich lived in England, but Hoffenberg, who had often entertained him in his house, eschewed any further contact with him.[28]

Martin Luther King

The National Union of South African Students (NUSAS) had an Advisory Panel whose membership included Professor Monica Wilson, Leo Marquard, Ernest Wentzel and Hoffenberg, and which dealt with many issues bearing on human rights. An annual lecture was named in honour of Professor T.B. Davie, a former Principal of the Cape Town University, who had been 'a fearless and forceful critic of apartheid and a defender of the principle of academic freedom'. Hoffenberg was commissioned to invite the great American civil rights campaigner, the Reverend Martin Luther King, to give the 1965 lecture. He wrote to King from England:

> The [Defence and Aid] Fund is motivated by its realization of the importance of the struggle in South Africa in terms of the cause of non-racialism through-out the world. We are gravely distressed at the direction taken by events in South Africa and believe that every avenue of non-violent protest must be fol-lowed; as in your own country, the role of students in South Africa is of major importance.

Martin Luther King responded, accepting the invitation. In June 1965 Hoffenberg wrote informing him that the committee in Cape Town would advise him about the visa problem:

> I personally, feel very pessimistic about your chances of getting a South African visa, but feel strongly that this should not deter you from trying! I know how much it would mean to all of us if you were able to come.

The outcome was negative and Luther King was unable to speak in South Africa before his assassination in 1968.[29]

The Defence and Aid Fund

The Defence and Aid Fund existed primarily to fund the defence of people accused of political crimes and misdemeanours, and to ameliorate the conditions of imprisoned political prisoners. Many black Africans lacked both resources for their defence and an understanding of the court system. The Fund was especially active in Cape Town, Durban and Johannesburg. Hoffenberg was prominent on its Management Committee and assumed its Chair in 1965, when John Blundell, the previous Chair, was deported. The following excerpts of letters from the Durban office to Cape Town indicate how the Fund gave support:

> Siegfried Bhengu. Accused of leaving country for military training. Pietermaritzburg Supreme Court case. Expected cost R300. Amelia Gasa and three others. Accused of furthering aims of banned ANC. Set down for Sept 27th. They are now out on bail and I have written to them giving name of lawyer ... We instructed our lawyer to go ahead with the two Robben Island cases, Joshua Zulu and Harry Gwala ... Our experience with Robben Island cases in the past indicates that if at all possible these should be defended, especially in view of the loss of study privileges which can result from a conviction...[30]

Hoffenberg had obtained assistance from Canon John Collins' Defence and Aid Fund (Christian Action) in London, as mentioned previously. His wife Diane visited Hoffenberg to discuss arrangements, and was staying with him on 2 November 1965 when early in the morning Security police called and impounded Hoffenberg's passport. Derek Hoffenberg, aged six, felt Security had shown insufficient respect for his father, and at breakfast declared trenchantly: 'Bloody shit police!' The spiritually minded Diane Collins said reassuringly: 'Quite right, Derek. Bloody shit police!'

Although the Fund was continually indebted for Collins' support, Hoffenberg was sometimes alarmed by Collins' indiscreet declarations in the Press and his association with communist organizations or groups which did not accept a non-violent constraint on their activities. His committee was therefore careful to distinguish itself as the South African Defence and Aid Fund. Its affairs prospered to the point where it could claim about an 80 per cent acquittal rate for its clients. This became altogether too much for the South African Government, which banned the Fund under the Suppression of Communism Act on 18 March 1966.[31]

It was risible to conceive that the Management Committee of the South African Defence and Aid Fund had any support for communism, since they were Establishment figures from the business and professional community and included people such as the society hostess Noël Robb. On 28 March the Committee decided to take legal action to get the ban revoked, but the

High Court found that the banning was legal. Hoffenberg sent a statement to the *Cape Times* denying any connection with communism and attacking the Minister for Justice's (B.J. Vorster) 'vague and unsubstantiated allegations'. Hoffenberg then took the case to the Supreme Court. On the 10 November 1966 the bench of five judges, in a split decision with the three Afrikaner judges in the majority, dismissed the appeal.[32]

The last of the Liberal Party

The South African Government never specifically banned the Liberal Party; it simply banned or imprisoned its leaders. Many members (including Hoffenberg in July 1964) had their homes searched and raided. The National Chairman of the Party, Peter Brown, was banned on 25 July 1964. Hoffenberg had immense respect and affection for Brown and his wife Phoebe; they lived modestly and gave most of their considerable wealth away. In *Contact* he was described as having:

> ... self-discipline, clarity of the spoken and written word ... and the ability to organize and lead ... His gifts of character, his honesty and his strength of purpose [enabled him] to inspire and sustain others ... [He had] a natural gift for communicating with people whose circumstances in life were very different from his own.[33]

Hoffenberg maintained his friendship with Brown until the latter's death in 2004. By this time Brown had established two self-sufficient Zulu farming communities on his land.

It was difficult for the Liberal Party to continue its normal activities from 1964 when many of its banned leaders went into exile. Former leaders, such as Margaret Ballinger, again assumed office and Hoffenberg attempted to keep *Contact* in press by inserting cuttings of overseas and local news reports which bore on the Party's objectives. The Party finally wound to its conclusion when on 9 May 1968 the Prohibition of Political Interference Bill became law; it became a criminal offence to belong to a multiracial political organization. Janet Robertson concluded her history of liberalism in South Africa thus:

> The white races in South Africa had been united by their common acceptance of a repressive policy towards non-whites. But loss of liberty for non-whites had inevitably meant loss of liberty for whites as well ... The determination to maintain white supremacy had proved incompatible with the maintenance of liberal principles.[34]

CHAPTER FIVE

Hoffenberg banned

The banning order

In 1967 P.C. Pelser, Minister for Justice issued, under the Suppression of Communism Act, a banning order on Hoffenberg which was to run for five years. Under it, he was to be confined to the magisterial districts of Wynberg and the Cape and barred from entering any educational premises; the latter restriction was not to apply until the end of the academic year. He was not to attend a gathering of more than two people and there were other constraints on communication, publishing and visiting sensitive areas such as harbours. Hoffenberg was to report to a police station each week.[1]

The banning of Hoffenberg caused a great and sustained public outcry; *The Cape Argus* declared that two doctors dominated the 1967 headlines: Hoffenberg and his banning, and Christian Barnard and his heart transplants. Naturally the immediate protest was at the University of Cape Town. After the news of Hoffenberg's restriction order was released on Sunday 30 July 1967, 500 medical students attended a protest meeting on the following Tuesday, and the steps of St George's cathedral were also occupied by students with posters. The Staff Association, the Students Representative Council and the Academic Freedom Committee of the University declared their outrage, and they were supported by the Independent Student Union, the acting-Chair of the University Council, Mr Frank Robb, and Margaret Marshall, President of NUSAS. Professor J.F. Brock condemned the ban 'forthrightly and with all the authority I can command ... speaking on behalf of some 76 specialists and some 50 non-specialized doctors of the division and department of medicine'. On the Friday about 1,600 students and staff crammed the Jameson Hall and heard messages of support for the protest from the diamond magnate H.F. Oppenheimer, Chancellor, and J.P. Duminy, Principal. A mass resignation of doctors at Groote Schuur Hospital was threatened.[2]

The other three English-language universities entered the fray but there was mainly silence from the Afrikaans-language universities, although a petition with 200 signatures emerged from Stellenbosch and a small joint protest came from the University of South Africa and Pretoria

University. There was an immediate protest from the University of Witwatersrand (Wits) where more than 100 students lined Jan Smuts Avenue; the Students Representative Council and the Academic Freedom Committee were vocal. About 400 students and staff of Rhodes University marched in academic dress through Grahamstown, where a plain clothes policeman was photographed in a niche of the cathedral wall, in the act of photographing all individuals in the procession. Staff at Natal University also opposed the ban on Hoffenberg.[3]

The wider community was involved: leaders of the Progressive Party, the Liberal Party, the Black Sash Movement, the South Africa Institute of Race Relations, and the National Council of Women of South Africa. An advertisement with more than 800 signatures which declared 'total opposition to the morally reprehensible practice of banning without prior trial' appeared in the Cape Town, Natal and Johannesburg newspapers; the signatories 'included 17 advocates and QCs, as well as leading figures in science, the arts and academic life'. Later 300 prominent citizens of Johannesburg protested whilst a subsequent petition to Pelser had more than 2,000 signatures.[4] Hoffenberg was continually followed by a black security car. One day, from a sense of mischief, he drove around a roundabout for fifteen minutes, until his pursuers took a side exit. Such a huge and spontaneous outcry of protest might have been expected to alter a Government decision, but not in the days of the intransigent Nationalist administration of 1967.

A diverse constituency

There were different emphases amongst the wide spectrum of support for Hoffenberg. Naturally friends and people who knew him rallied in his defence. To Dr L.C. Isaacson he was 'a gentle man and a dedicated humanitarian', to Professor W.P.U. Jackson 'my closest and most valued colleague', whilst Bernard Pimstone commented that 'his stand on the liberty of the individual is surely the very antithesis of doctrinaire communism'. Anthony Delius wrote a long article about 'My Friend, Bill Hoffenberg', describing his family background in Port Elizabeth, his sporting and academic achievements at the Grey High School and the University of Cape Town, and his patriotic service with a tank regiment in North Africa and Italy. His medical research had made him a world figure, and he 'taught with abounding energy and enthusiasm'. His passion for justice had led him to support the Defence and Aid Fund, but 'Bill Hoffenberg had never in his life wittingly connived at aiding to achieve the aims of communism'. Helen Suzman, from the rival Progressive Party, wrote: 'I am ... convinced that Dr Hoffenberg is no communist and that his main concern has been the attainment of a just society in South Africa, because he is a humanitarian and a man of compassion.'[5]

The second main defensive thrust concerned the banning under the Suppression of Communism Act. Hoffenberg himself wished the protests to focus wholly on the general use of the restriction order; he was No. 683, and a lot of banned, powerless people required support. The paramount need was to overturn the extra-judicial system that allowed a minister to sign an order prepared by an anonymous official which could not be appealed in court. The minister did not need to give reasons for his action; although this was contrary 'to the requirements of justice, democracy and good government'. Pelser refused to give the grounds for the restriction order on Hoffenberg who many protesters urged should face the courts or some impartial tribunal to determine his guilt or innocence. Pelser stated:

> If we have deviated from certain legal procedures it has been done for a very sound and good reason. We have done it to deal with those persons who wish to further the aims of communism and to undermine the country ... *All we have done has been to prevent these people from using legal machinery to defeat the ends of justice* [author's italics].[6]

This was indeed a remarkable statement, supporting the critics who believed South Africa had become a Police state.

The third polemic concerned the defence of academic freedom and the autonomy of universities. Leo Marquard wrote

> ...the government of the Republic is anti-intellectual ... The concept of academic freedom was dealt three severe blows by Mr B.J. Vorster's Government...: Dr Raymond Hoffenberg was banned, Prof. Clark Kerr, of the United States of America, was refused a visa to enter South Africa, and Mr & Mrs John Daniel were refused passports to go to America for further study.

These incidents were seen as 'a renewed attempt ... to intimidate the English-language universities'. The former Principal, T.B. Davie, was quoted as defining academic freedom as including 'the right to decide who shall teach'. Lord James of the University of York, lecturing at Wits University, saw Hoffenberg's banning as an attack on academic freedom: 'Universities had a particular responsibility as champions of essential liberties by reason of the intellectual strength which they possess and the intellectual integrity they defend.'[7]

A letter to B.J. Vorster signed by 188 medical students stated that 'at no time has Dr Hoffenberg expressed any political opinions in his lectures'. A teach-in on 'Freedom, the State and the Rule of Law' attracted 400 Cape Town students. The Nationalist Government hoped a conformist society would adopt Afrikaner mores; there was 'the danger of the

University acceding to a value-system condemned by its counterparts throughout the world'. At Wits the Academic Freedom Committee complained:

> A scholar had been prevented from publishing the fruits of his research, South African scholarship had lost his published work, and a university had effectively been deprived of the right to continue the appointment of one of its teachers.

Pelser, when challenged, stated: 'There was no restriction preventing Dr Hoffenberg from preparing and disseminating any document or publication of a purely medical-scientific nature.'[8] Hoffenberg's prohibited access to a university library or laboratory did not augur well for his future science.

A fourth area of concern was the loss of Hoffenberg to medical science in South Africa. Even before his banning the removal of his passport had impeded his work. He was unable to attend an International Atomic Energy Agency meeting in Vienna; the Agency said a research programme on protein metabolism and protein depletion involving nine nations would be seriously handicapped. Clearly Hoffenberg had strong support in Vienna. The *Sunday Times* reported:

> Recently the South African Government refused to forward his application for a renewal of funds to the International Atomic Energy Agency on the grounds that he had been chairman of a banned organization (Defence and Aid Fund). The Agency, however, insisted on making the grant to the University of Cape Town's Department of Medicine, provided that Dr Hoffenberg remained its senior investigator.[9]

Some 14 leading Medical Specialists at Groote Schuur wrote to the Press expressing support for the value of Hoffenberg's medical work, and the protests from overseas indicated the high regard for his medical standing. In the London *Times* there were letters of support from 14 medical professors of the universities of Oxford, London, Nottingham and Belfast and 24 South African postgraduate medical students, and earlier letters from Professor J.C. Waterlow and other UK scientists. The *British Medical Journal* published a leading article: 'By its actions the Department of Justice has effectively deprived the world of medicine ...' From the United States and Canada, 45 medical men who held professorships or other significant posts referred to Hoffenberg's 'achievements as clinician, teacher and research worker'.[10]

By contrast Hoffenberg was deeply disappointed that his professional organization did not support him: J.F. Brock reported that 'the Medical Association [of South Africa] does not wish to comment upon a matter which is regarded by approximately half of its members as a political rather than a professional matter'. Hoffenberg believed office bearers who were also members of the Broederbond influenced this outcome.[11]

The final expression of concern related to the effect of the ban in accelerating the brain drain from South Africa, in exacerbating the problems of future recruitment from overseas and in diminishing South Africa's international standing. The *Sunday Times* reported that 'some of South Africa's leading medical teachers and researchers will quit the country next year as a result of the banning of Dr Raymond Hoffenberg'. Professor Phillip Tobias believed many postgraduate students studying overseas did 'not return because of increasing Government interference with our non-nationalist universities', whilst the *Cape Times* referred to 'the serious effects upon this country's recruitment of desperately needed medical and other professional skills'. J. Hamilton Russell, returning from a business trip through Europe, North America and the Far East, noted Hoffenberg headlines as far afield as Singapore and Japan and adverse comment about South Africa throughout the world.[12]

The University of Cape Town sought a meeting with Pelser. He responded by asking for a written statement concerning the administrative matters they wished to discuss. The deputation consisted of H.F. Oppenheimer, Chancellor, J.P. Duminy, Principal, C.S. Corder, Chairman of Council, and J.F. Brock. Margaret Hoffenberg, who had to act as Hoffenberg's spokesperson throughout the controversy, said:

> I sincerely hope that, after all this, the deputation will not go to the Minister to ask for a few concessions. The Minister by now should know that my husband would accept nothing short of the complete lifting of the ban. Alternatively my husband is fully prepared to face any court or impartial tribunal which the Minister might set up to examine the reasons for the banning notice. My husband would prefer to continue his work in this country, which, after all, is the place of his birth. But he will certainly not do so unless the ban is lifted entirely.

The deputation spent 75 minutes with Pelser on 19 October 1967; the Minister reserved his decision.[13]

The reason why

We now know the reasons the South African Government gave for banning Hoffenberg, since in 2004 he obtained a copy of his Security file, which contained more than 700 pages.[14] It indicates he was under continual intrusive surveillance: physical observation, phone tapping and mail tampering. Over the period September 1962 to April 1967, 58 incidents in his

Derek (left) and
Peter Hoffenberg
with their parents,
early 1968.

life are detailed, and these formed the basis of the case against him. Initially
it was planned to ban him in April 1966, but the decision was postponed
until his role in the Defence and Aid Fund appeals against its suppression,
made to the High Court and the Supreme Court, had been ended.

The first category of concern noted in the Security file was his active
support for organizations which were unpopular with the Nationalist
Government but all of which were organizations that at that time had a
legal entity. His work and gifts to the Defence and Aid Fund, which
essentially helped to assist the court defence of accused persons, an
inalienable right under South African law, attracted eight entries on his
file. Hoffenberg's attempt to form the College of Adult Education and
Training in Bechuanaland (Botswana), which was supported by Sir
Seretse Khama and the UK Government Minister, Mrs Eirene White,
attracted especial opprobrium; the advancement of black Africans as
informed political leaders in society had no place in the Nationalist
Government's restricted goals for black education. There were ten entries
concerning his support for the Liberal Party and its newspaper *Contact*.

His involvements in the South African Institute of Race Relations and
the Black Sash movement were mentioned; somewhat surprisingly his

membership of the Board of Kupugani, which worked simply to improve the nutrition of the community, also appeared in his file. Amnesty International and the Civil Rights League attracted notice, the latter from a misunderstood tapped phone call. Security (Kompol) was especially concerned by his advisory role to the National Union of South African Students (NUSAS) and their attempt to invite 'a certain person' (Martin Luther King) to South Africa.

The second category of concern was public activity considered antipathetic to the Nationalist Government: attendance at a demonstration against the Suppression of Communism Act, involvement with other medical professionals in the petition against solitary confinement, and the writing of an article in the *Sunday Times* about maltreatment of prisoners. Also logged was his unsuccessful attempt to promote the writer Leo Marquard for the position of Chancellor of the University of Cape Town.

The final category was the usual last refuge of Security accusation: guilt by association. There were various grades of suspicious companionship, ranging from lunch with the US Consul, having Alan Paton or Peter Brown to stay in his home, consorting with Barbara Castle, a member of the British Labour party, in London, to being in contact with 'the listed communist' Sonia Bunting. Meetings with two members of the African Resistance Movement, John Lang and Neville Rubin, were noted but it was conceded that 'nothing of safety importance was discussed'. Hoffenberg had attended mixed race social gatherings where 'there were no political speeches'.

His association with a further half dozen radicals was listed, and Security noted 'from a delicate source' that he had visited and given money to a Coloured man, George Peake. Hoffenberg commented:

> George Peake was house-arrested after serving a prison sentence. I used to visit him occasionally to keep him company as he saw very few people; the money came from my own pocket as he had no income at all and was unable to work. I learned later that during his internment his [Coloured] wife started an affair with one of the [white] Security police; his wife was obviously 'the delicate source'.[15]

Hoffenberg's Security File contained no reference to any criminal activity, but nevertheless the Security (Kompol) recommendation was:

> It appears that since 1962 Raymond Hoffenberg has been in touch with listed persons and known leftists. From the nature of his utterances it is clear that he pursues leftist objectives and can easily influence students. By identifying himself with these objectives he is furthering the aims of communism and is lucky that steps have not been taken against him earlier. We therefore recommend banning and cessation of his work as a lecturer. His income should not be affected as he can still practise as a doctor.

This recommendation can only be understood by recognizing Security's stance on communism as being primarily concerned with a non-racialist agenda. The value of Hoffenberg's role in medical research and his international status in medical science was completely discounted in formulating it's views on him. No evidence was presented that his teaching had promoted communism. Hoffenberg stated that he had been careful to avoid any political references in his teaching, but conceded that he had been courteous in referring to black patients as 'Mr' and 'Mrs'.[16] Rather than an indictment of Hoffenberg's misdemeanours, the file describes an exemplar for a concerned human rights advocate: thoughtful, committed, compassionate and non-violent.

The fallout

Pelser was unmoved by the representations made to him by the University deputation and communicated his intransigence to the Council of the University, which nevertheless 'reiterated its grave disquiet about the restriction order'. Brock issued a long statement affirming the need to protect the Republic's security, but declaring that 'nothing [the Minister for Justice] has said has given me any reason to believe that [the banning] is justifiable in this sense'. Duminy said: 'I personally know nothing that I can regard as grounds for the action taken against him,' Pelser's decision was front page news across the English-language newspapers, the subject of fierce adverse comment throughout the world, and evoked protest from a meeting of 100 doctors at Groote Schuur. It was decided to establish a lecture on a medical or scientific topic at the University of Cape Town to commemorate Hoffenberg and his banning. A series of protests continued in South Africa until his departure.[17]

Hoffenberg had unsolicited offers of employment in the UK, USA, Canada, Australia and Jamaica. Seven of his former associates at the New End Hospital in Hampstead, London, including Raymond Greene, urged in the *British Medical Journal* that 'a professorial or senior consultant post should be created for him at once' in Britain. In the interim Hoffenberg continued as a senior physician at the Groote Schuur Hospital until the end of 1967, and was the doctor who declared the second heart transplant donor ready for the surgeon Christian Barnard (as described in chapter 10). Margaret Hoffenberg meanwhile was the butt of many threatening phone calls from neighbours who supported the ban, and from Security. Hoffenberg focused on writing up his PhD for the University of Cape Town on protein metabolism and depletion; his research assistant, Elizabeth Black (who later was to work with him in England) visited the University Library to bring him any material he lacked at his home.[18]

Departure from South Africa. Over 2,000 students came to the airport on
28 March 1968 when Bill left for England.

In February 1968 the Hoffenbergs were allowed a 10-day visa to visit
Britain and to attend appointment committees. Hoffenberg accepted two
positions: as Senior Scientist of the Medical Research Council, Division of
Biophysics at Mill Hill, and as Consultant Physician (Endocrinology) at
the New End Hospital. The Mill Hill group at the National Institute of
Medical Research was headed by Sir Peter Medawar and these significant
positions would enable Hoffenberg to continue his clinical and research
career in institutions at the forefront of British medical science. Upon his
return to Cape Town he was granted a single exit visa, which carried the
threat of imprisonment were he ever again to enter South Africa.[19]

So the Hoffenbergs reluctantly leased their beautiful home at
Bishopscourt for five years and arranged to leave Cape Town on 28 March
1968. Hoffenberg was driven to the D.F. Malan Airport by Max
Durbach, whilst Margaret and the two boys travelled with his cousin
René Durbach. They were bidden farewell by about 2,000 people:

> Medical students in white coats lined up on lawns behind the tarmac fence.
> The overflow gathered on the upstairs balcony and in the foyer of the termi-
> nal hall. Many of the students wore graduate and undergraduate gowns.
> Members of the Black Sash, who had earlier demonstrated with placards at
> the top of Adderley Street, joined the crowd wearing black arm-bands. Many
> relatives and friends of the Hoffenberg family also awaited their arrival.

A contingent of about 15 uniformed police as well as security police [with dogs on leashes] ... stood by watching.

Margaret Hoffenberg made a brief speech of thanks while a sole police photographer took pictures of the crowd.

At 2.45 pm, a few minutes before passengers were asked to board the aircraft, a medical student called for three cheers. The crowd broke into applause, then began singing the South African national anthem, 'Die Stem'. On the tarmac Dr and Mrs Hoffenberg turned to face the crowd and stood at attention until the song ended. Dr Hoffenberg, clearly overwhelmed, held up his hand in farewell.[20]

Clive McBride, a black clergyman friend, called out: 'Bill, we will overcome.' This was immediately taken up by the crowd who immediately burst into that great civil rights song 'We Shall Overcome'. As the aircraft flew north over the veld Hoffenberg had no way of knowing that it would be nearly 24 years before he could return to South Africa, and 26 years until Nelson Mandela's multiracial government would rule South Africa.[21]

CHAPTER SIX

Birmingham

Return to academe

In 1972 the William Withering Chair of Medicine and the Headship of the Department of Medicine at Birmingham University were vacant. Graham Bull, who had been Hoffenberg's first clinical tutor in South Africa, suggested Hoffenberg as a candidate to Owen Wade, then Professor of Therapeutics and Clinical Pharmacology. He invited Hoffenberg to Birmingham; Robert Hunter, the Vice Chancellor, was displeased by Wade's initiative, but in the event Hoffenberg, having made a late *pro forma* application, was interviewed one lunch-time and received an offer in the post next morning.

So the Hoffenbergs moved to Birmingham. They acquired Shepherd's Yard, a large three-storey, double-fronted Georgian rectory with stone floors at Kinwarton, some 40 kilometres from the University. The dovecote in the garden had been designated a National Trust heritage site. There was a tennis court, and Hoffenberg also played squash and tennis at the Edgbaston Club. As the house was only 13 kilometres from Stratford-upon-Avon, the Hoffenbergs were able to go often to the Royal Shakespeare Theatre, but work pressures eventually caused Hoffenberg to give up golf. Hoffenberg preferred to live in the country. He did not mind driving and usually started for work early, returning late when the roads were clear. When his sons, Derek and Peter, outgrew their preparatory school they moved as weekly boarders to Warwick School; their father would collect them on Saturday mornings and drive them home for the weekend.

Hoffenberg was welcomed to his first Faculty Board meeting on 9 October 1972.[1] In his naivety he had not set conditions upon his acceptance of the Chair or declared a future plan for his Department, which had two spacious floors for laboratories but little else. He went cap in hand to the Dean, William Trethowan, to ask for funds to refurbish the laboratories and for approval of his long shopping list for equipment. Trethowan agreed to Hoffenberg's design of the proposed refurbishment and to his equipment requirements. After two years Hoffenberg had established an excellent endocrine unit. Michael Fitzgerald and the surgeon Geoffrey Oates joined him in an endocrine clinic. He brought Elizabeth Black, who had been his research assistant at Groote Schuur, to the laboratory and recruited David Ramsden, subsequently to become Reader in Medicine, from his old team at Northwick Park. A post was created for Michael Sheppard, a brilliant student from Hoffenberg's South African stable, who was eventually an eminent occupant of the William Withering Chair. The group later worked closely with the NHS endocrine unit headed by David London.[2] London was eventually to become Registrar at the Royal College of Physicians.

Head of department

In 1972, the Department of Medicine at Birmingham had a wide remit: in addition to a responsibility for teaching general and clinical practice it embraced cardiology, rheumatology, oncology, endocrinology, respiratory disease, gastroenterology and renal medicine. Hoffenberg enunciated his general approach in a wide-ranging Inaugural Lecture, '*Tria Juncta in Uno*: The Role of the Academic Medical Unit'. The stated mission of the university was the acquisition, transmission and application of knowledge: 'The dominance of the endpoint distinguished medicine from most other university subjects and explained, in part at least, the preoccupation with methods of teaching and with the control and quality of research.' He argued that 'the knowledge and modes of thought acquired during the pre-clinical years formed the only secure basis of clinical practice … clinical medicine is simply applied biological science'.

Hoffenberg believed that research had a central role in a medical unit; he expanded on this theme:

> As a general rule the best teachers are those who've had research experience, and those who lack it usually lack lustre as teachers … Time spent in a laboratory … teaches us a great deal about technical processes and reproducibility and especially about biological variability, thus reinforcing our appreciation of the uniqueness of the individual and his [or her] response to disease.
>
> A further virtue of research is that it carries you across boundaries, again bringing home to one the continuum of knowledge from chemistry, physics and mathematics, through biochemistry, physiology, pathology to medicine … At various times I've had to learn something about techniques as diverse as thyroid scanning and whole body counting, radioimmunoassay, protein fractionation, electrophoresis, all forms of chromatography, mass spectrometry, the use of computers, biomathematical modelling and compartment analysis, not to mention measuring exoxphthalmos in a gold fish or collecting an accurate 24-hour urine specimen from a male rabbit …

Hoffenberg reviewed different models of medical teaching and research and argued that the increasing specialization in medicine made it all the more necessary to have an academic unit in a teaching hospital which would provide 'a nucleus of enthusiasts prepared to take on a continuing responsibility'. He suggested:

> If these super-specialties are to be linked, like spokes of a wheel radiating out from a central hub, one must ensure that the hub is the strongest part; loss of one or more spokes need not impair the movement of a wheel, loss of its hub will cause it instantly to collapse. An educational focal point is needed, disciplined not to abandon the basic principles of medical education in favour of esotericism. The entrenchment of this fundamental approach should be facilitated by links with basic science and other university departments ... to provide a genuine multidisciplinary approach to teaching and, of course, to research ... The constant exposure of the scientist to clinical problems and of the clinician to the methods and thought processes of science ... will most effectively bring about the confluence of basic and applied research.
>
> Far from being moribund, then, I picture the medical unit as active, energetic ... ecumenical and expanded.[3]

Hoffenberg was to pursue this central polemic for the Department of Medicine during his 13 years at Birmingham. His style might be described as directed to a guided collegiality. He listened to everybody, was courteous, humorous and charming, inspired considerable loyalty from his staff, but somehow usually achieved his own objectives for the Department. His smiling exterior, likened by one failed student to a gold plate on the coffin, did not belie his rigorous standards, his acute perception of the realities of present situations, and his underlying determination. On his arrival in Birmingham he encountered resentment and

Hosting a laboratory party with Elizabeth Black at the Department of Medicine, University of Birmingham.

entrenched situations not to his liking. Ann Cowell – his personal secretary, who continued to work with him later at the Royal College of Physicians and at Wolfson College – noted that after bruising discussions, Hoffenberg, frustrated but calm, would dictate to her a confidential record of outcomes for his own use. Seated at his desk, he would transfer his thoughts into a fast stream of words, perfectly structured into a logical sequence. His very full appointments diary was kept meticulously, so that he could be located readily, and he made himself always accessible in his office.[4]

Collegiality was strengthened by social activity. Once a month about 20 staff and students came for drinks at Kinwarton and the Hoffenbergs were also generous with dinner parties, although Margaret had minimal domestic help. Once each year families walked in the Malvern Hills, stopped at a pub for lunch, and ended up for dinner at Kinwarton, where the Persian rugs were inverted against children's ice cream.

The introduction of medical audit

Whilst Elizabeth Black organised the smooth running of his laboratory, Hoffenberg devoted himself more fully to clinical work and became a consultant to the Birmingham East Health District. The improvement of standards of clinical treatment was Hoffenberg's continual preoccupation at Queen Elizabeth Hospital. He believed that self-regulation of the medical profession was likely to be a much more effective approach to raising standards of care than intrusive external supervision, which usually became directed to cost-saving measures rather than improving patient welfare.

Ann Cowell, Bill's secretary at Birmingham who continued to work with him in this role at The Royal College of Physicians and later at Wolfson College.

A group of his colleagues were prepared to embark upon regular peer review of their routine work and in 1977, David Heath, Reader in Medicine, took the initiative in devising a pro forma for reviewing the treatment of a sample of patients.[5] Owen Wade, was another early proponent of the scheme, which was supported by Hoffenberg, John Bishop and Martin Kendall.

This group, together with junior colleagues and senior students, met weekly in the lunch-hour, and had open and frank discussion on the treatment of patients. At one of the meetings all deaths that had occurred in the previous month would be reviewed with respect to patient management and whether the deaths might have been avoided. Other meetings took random samples of discharged patient notes to review whether the initial medical notes had been adequate, the later course of the illness well documented, and whether the investigations had been appropriate or unnecessary. The suitability of the initial treatment and of the use of drugs were also reviewed, and communication with the patient, the relatives and the general practitioner after the patient's discharge was assessed. Gradually the exercise grew until about one-quarter of discharged patient notes were reviewed. Junior staff needed little encouragement to criticize the decisions of senior staff – often a humbling experience for god-professors. Hoffenberg wrote:

> The main benefit of the weekly meetings was educational. The knowledge that their management of a patient might be discussed openly and in detail led both consultants and junior staff to think more critically about their decisions. At the audit meeting they could expect to be challenged and to have to provide reasonable explanations for their actions. The need to justify one's actions led to a more thoughtful use of investigations and treatment. Whether a decision was correct or not was considered less important than the fact that it could be justified … The important outcome of audit was an acceptance of the need to be accountable.[6]

Further consequences of these meetings were the great improvement in the quality of note-taking, in the records of the information given to patients, and in the speed with which a final discharge letter was sent to the GP. The introduction of regular medical audits at Queen Elizabeth Hospital was seminal, and in later years the practice was widely adopted (as discussed in chapter 8). The concept and practice of audit was received most enthusiastically in university hospitals, but some consultants felt threatened by criticism and would excuse themselves on the grounds that their efficient management of time left little space for this type of discussion.

Medical education

The Faculty of Medicine and Dentistry involved Hoffenberg in several working parties; he joined the Executive in 1973. His attempts to revise the undergraduate curriculum met only with partial success. He favoured teaching in small groups and the early exposure of students to clinical experience, but some consultants were loath to give time to junior undergraduates. He was however successful in introducing case studies to a jointly taught biochemistry course. To Jayne Franklyn, whom he coached for her MRCP exams, he was an inspiring teacher, combining charisma and presence with academic authority. Hoffenberg made himself available for student counselling; a box of tissues was a necessary office accoutrement to questions such as 'Would you rather be a long-distance truck driver and not have to do the work?' He made a practice of seeking out perhaps 20 students in each year, focusing on the top and the bottom of academic success. Continuous assessment, both from essays and other tests and from staff gradings, was expanded. Student presentations were well rehearsed.

His main achievement was to increase the number of teaching hospitals in Birmingham, something which did not suit many consultants with an entrenched practice. Students could use the Queen Elizabeth, the General, and Children and Women's hospitals, but Hoffenberg believed they were not exposed to a sufficiently broad case mix and received inadequate supervision. At a Faculty Board meeting in May 1974 he gained approval for a one-year trial of teaching at the Selly Oak, East Birmingham and Dudley Road hospitals; once started he did not return to the Faculty for further endorsement. His plan was that at each hospital there would be a senior lecturer of the University in charge of clinical teaching; Ian Green, Anthony Barnett and Gareth Beevers were initially responsible for the newly enrolled hospitals and Alex Wright for the General Hospital; later the Good Hope Hospital was included. By the time medical undergraduate intake had increased from 160 in 1973 to 350 in 2003, some 13 teaching hospitals were involved.[7]

The lack of resources available for teaching general practice was a continual problem. In January 1980 Hoffenberg pointed out there was a single staff member, Dr Robin Hull, and secretarial services provided by the Department of Medicine; no funds were available for further part-time lecturers and the remuneration paid to GPs taking students barely covered their expenses. Instead of embarking upon costly new ventures the Faculty might remedy existing deficiencies. Early in the following year (Sir) Michael Drury was elected to a Chair in general practice which marked a turning point in GP education.[8]

Hoffenberg served on the Higher Degrees Committee from 1978 and attracted many students from overseas. Babatunde Osotimehin from Nigeria 'a lovely man', developed a good thyroglobulin assay and obtained a PhD and an MRCP, and became Minister of Health in Nigeria. William Makgoba from South Africa gained top marks in his MRCP exams and did clinical research with Hoffenberg for two years before taking a senior lectureship at Imperial College. After many vicissitudes he became Vice-Chancellor of the University of Natal. The talented Jayne Franklyn added lustre to his group; she went on to become Professor of Medicine in the Division of Medical Sciences at Birmingham.

As an examiner for the MD and the more supervised PhD, Hoffenberg had stringent standards, usually but not always aligned with his co-examiners. He failed one MD candidate: 'I do not think that we should accept work of lower standard simply on the grounds that it was performed under difficult conditions.' He had high standards for the use of language; one MD candidate who although displaying a good level of research alarmed Hoffenberg by his spelling and grammatical errors: 'Before this thesis is placed on the shelves, the author should be encouraged to go through it with a dictionary and delete the evidence of illiteracy.' The Department of Medicine had a greater commitment to PhD education (6–7 candidates in 1982–83) than other departments in the Faculty (maximum 2 candidates).[9]

Extramural links

The Medical Faculty had an organic association with the Godfrey Huggins School of Medicine in Salisbury (Harare), Southern Rhodesia (Zimbabwe), which was severed in November 1975; but the question of retaining further links was canvassed. Ian Smith's illegal regime was an anathema to Hoffenberg and he successfully persuaded the University Senate to sever relations completely until the regime changed. However, the plight of medical students overseas who had been forced to abandon their courses because of political or racial discrimination drew his sympathy, and in May 1977 he successfully proposed that students in such exceptional circumstances be given permission for clinical attachments of one year or more to study for Conjoint Board Examinations at Birmingham.[10]

In Britain Hoffenberg developed strong professional links beyond Birmingham, especially in science publishing. He had joined the Board of the journal *Clinical Science* shortly after arriving from South Africa. He became friendly with its editor, Tristram Freeman, who, on his death bed, asked Hoffenberg to take over the editorship, which Hoffenberg did in 1971. The Biochemical Society and the Medical Research Society held a joint financial interest in the journal. Hoffenberg changed the financial arrangements, revolutionized the speed of publication so that the journal became more attractive to research scientists, and thereby he generated profits. His association with this journal also allowed him contact with medical scientists throughout Britain. The Medical Research Society used to meet monthly at different medical schools, usually attended only by those who presented papers. When Hoffenberg assumed the Chair in 1978 he and Ken Saunders reorganized matters; the Society met twice each year, funded the attendance of young scientists submitting papers and became a very popular and sociable organization.

The *Quarterly Journal of Medicine* had a small, largely self-appointed Board of six members. In 1975 Hoffenberg became editor and enlarged the Board to ensure better referencing of papers, appointed a new publisher and generated sufficient profits to enable a fellowship for overseas doctors to be funded. The previous emphasis on rather discursive review articles shifted to research papers swiftly published, and the 'Quarterly' appeared monthly.

The Association of Physicians, founded by William Osler in 1905, is an élite group which then admitted no more than twelve new members each year. It met annually at regional centres over two days to discuss a highly selected collection of papers; Hoffenberg joined its Executive Committee in 1977.

His membership of the Medical Research Council was more demanding and continued from 1978 until 1982. He had previously been an adviser dealing with biological systems and regarded the MRC as a good, fair organization. It had a huge agenda, supporting research by awarding grants across the entire spectrum of medical sciences. Each grant request – whether for comparatively small short-term projects or major 10-year programmes of research – was subject to a detailed review. The experience he gained in working with the MRC and other medical scientific bodies provided a useful background for his later role of President of the Royal College of Physicians to which he was elected in 1983.

The Birmingham legacy

The high standing that Birmingham University enjoys in the medical world may be illustrated by the fact that in 1983 three Presidents of Royal Colleges – Geoffrey Slaney for the Surgeons, Professor Robert Curran for the Pathologists and Hoffenberg for the Physicians – were staff members at Birmingham; this happy circumstance was celebrated at a grand dinner in June 1983. The concurrent demands of the Royal College Presidency and the Headship of the Department of Medicine eventually became too great for Hoffenberg, so that he retired from Birmingham in 1985, aged 62 years. By this time his endocrine research group had attained international recognition and Hoffenberg had moved the younger research workers towards molecular biology. His Department had educated many medical scientists who attained eminence. Some have already been mentioned. Julian Davis became Professor of Endocrinology, Peter Bayliss, Dean of Medicine at the University of Newcastle-upon-Tyne, Steven Franks, Professor of Reproductive Medicine at Imperial College, London, and Kevin Doherty, Professor of Biochemistry at Aberdeen, whilst Richard Clayton occupied the Chair of Medicine at Keele. At Birmingham Gareth Beevers, Bob Stockley and Jo Bradwell all achieved Chairs. Many, for example Anthony Barnett at the Heartlands Diabetes Unit, became leading NHS consultants, whilst Bill Burr, a close colleague of Hoffenberg's, became a Postgraduate Dean in Yorkshire. Some went overseas, such as John Marshall, who became Chief of Medicine at the University of Virginia. Anthony Zalin, a gifted lecturer, returned to full-time medical practice and became a consultant at Stourbridge. This by no means exclusive list illustrates Hoffenberg's success as a university teacher and needs to be set alongside the considerable affection in which he was held by his patients, his students and his staff.[11]

CHAPTER SEVEN

Wolfson College, Oxford

Prelude

Linked to the River Cherwell in North Oxford by two narrow cuttings, there is an artificial harbour enclosed by two wings of Wolfson College. The southern wing which curves gently to the river was to have been straight, but Sir Isaiah Berlin – the first President of the College and a leading liberal thinker of the twentieth century – wanted to echo the curve of the harbour at Portofino where he had a house. He bombarded the architects with postcards of the Portofino harbour until they agreed to change their original design. The Wolfson water meadows across the river, and the mature trees, once part of the estate of the scientist J.S. Haldane, provide a more pastoral setting than is possible for the undergraduate colleges of crowded central Oxford. Haldane's house was demolished to make way for the modern, 'international' style Wolfson, which was opened in 1974; its style is typical of its time, having strong horizontal lines of glass and exposed aggregate. There is no senior common room and the dining hall, in which there is no high table, is square – a sign of the Wolfson egalitarianism – and has a lofty, tent-like ceiling.

Wolfson College, together with St Cross, was established as a 'college of entitlement' for dons who otherwise lacked a college affiliation.[1] Originally, called Iffley College when founded in 1965, it was renamed Wolfson College in 1966 after Sir Isaac Wolfson. Sir Isaac had donated £1.5 million to match a grant from the Ford Foundation, secured by McGeorge Bundy who had collaborated with Isaiah Berlin in wartime intelligence.

The College governance is democratic, with students and research fellows alike represented on the Governing Body and committees. The students, some 550, are all postgraduate, so the College ambience is spared the wilder excesses typical of younger undergraduates. There is a strong emphasis on international recruitment, overseas students coming from more than 60 countries; in 1985 they constituted about one-third of the student body. At that time about two-thirds of students read physical or biological science, and one-third humanities or social science; 30 per cent were

Wolfson College, Oxford with the harbour in the foreground.

women. To these should be added a large membership of the Common Room and about 200 fellows – Governing Body, Supernumerary, Emeritus, Honorary, Research, Junior Research and Visiting – the whole making up a diverse, mature academic community.[2] Wolfson College was unusual in that a child care centre was incorporated into the design when the present buildings were occupied in 1974. Students could even grow their own vegetables and flowers on the College allotments.

A new President

Sir Henry Fisher, who had succeeded Isaiah Berlin as College President, retired in 1985. By the end of 1984 the College had elected a successor but he declined the appointment. James Mann, supported by Basil Shepstone, suggested Hoffenberg should be approached.[3] Hoffenberg had been finding his dual roles as President of the Royal College of Physicians and Head of the Department of Medicine at Birmingham University too demanding and had decided he would retire from Birmingham in 1985. However, the headship of an Oxford College is often regarded as a part-time occupation; duties may be devolved and a college accepts the reflected glow from the public activities of a distinguished *persona*. A small group of fellows were deputed to meet

Hoffenberg in London, and he and Margaret then visited Wolfson. Mann, Derek Wyatt, Julian Roberts and Nick Allen were their hosts.

Hoffenberg was invited to meet the Governing Body. He sat in a chair opposite more than 50 fellows, and was a little surprised to find himself being questioned for more than an hour about his attitudes to research, academia and sport. A particularly egregious fellow, designated 'The Young Nero' by Sir Ronald Syme, sat in the front row and was especially persistent with his questioning. At this point Hoffenberg considered withdrawing,[4] but as the proportion of assenting smiles at Hoffenberg's responses increased, it was clear the Governing Body was eager for him to accept the position. His appointment, which was to take effect in October 1985, and his resignation from Birmingham, were announced to the Faculty of Medicine and Dentistry on 25 February 1985.[5]

In some respects this was an unusual appointment. Hoffenberg was a complete outsider in Oxford, and needed education in the Byzantine labyrinth of hierarchical decision making and committee structures of the University. By many he was welcomed as a breath of fresh air, a bridge between generations, a South African outside the English class system.[6] The College accepted him on his own terms, recognizing his extra-mural

Wolfson College Presidents. (*Left to right*) Sir David Smith, Bill, Sir Isaiah Berlin and Sir Henry Fisher, 1994.

responsibilities, particularly his presidency of the Royal College of Physicians in which role he continued until 1989. In Oxford, heads of colleges have only the power they are skilful enough to acquire through the consent of the fellows. On some occasions it became clear Hoffenberg found this a difficult transition from his former roles where his authority was less trammelled. Although a minority of fellows were suspicious of the latent medical god-professor who had come among them, the majority found Hoffenberg approachable, charming and a good listener.

So the Hoffenbergs moved into the President's Lodgings, a large Victorian house in Chadlington Road with a rear entrance to the College garden. As the house was unfurnished, the Hoffenbergs decided to move in their furniture and to sell their Georgian rectory at Kinwarton. The Governing Body was pleased by the modest nature of their request for minor refurbishment to provide easier access to the individual bedrooms.[7] Hoffenberg wrote:

> The installation of the new Vice-Chancellor [of Oxford University] on my first day in office seemed designed to imprint the romantic image of Oxford. The ceremony itself, the leisurely procession to All Souls to the background of church bells on a particularly beautiful day, an excellent lunch and the subsequent dispersal of black-gowned dons on bicycles seemed all too familiar. Oxford was playing to the gallery – and in sparkling form. I now know that such occasions are rare and there is more serious business to be done …
>
> Of course, the Wolfson buildings provide the most striking first impression: the rather austere Central [later Berlin] Quad (does it need a touch of colour – a bougainvillea or two?); the successful softening of cold architectural geometry in the Tree Quad; the beauty of the harbour, especially from my office; the unexpected glimpses of greenery through cleverly placed windows; the warmth and loftiness of the dining hall, an unusually depressing area in most university residences I have known. I thought at first the buildings were rather too severe, but they – or I – seem to have mellowed over the months. The garden, too, tends to hide its light under a bushel, and it took a formal Garden Tour to infect us with some of Walter Sawyer's enthusiasm and a better appreciation of his vision for the future.[8]

College living

The community life that had evolved at Wolfson catered for a diversity of interests: art, drama, Christianity, music, bridge, Linnaean studies, Tai Chi, wine and other eclectic pursuits. The Hoffenbergs helped to found a gastronomical society. They took their obligations for hospitality seriously. Dinner parties for ten or twelve (including wives) were held in their home until all new students had visited them; this helped their sense of belonging to the College. Special lunches in College catered for visiting fellows and new staff members. Wolfson people still speak of the Hoffenbergs' lively parties, where it was said that the pitch of noise surrounding Hoffenberg tended to the upper register, since he was popular with women and encouraged their interests.[9] There would be a garden party for the Governing Body and senior staff, a luncheon for the secretaries and a Christmas party for the children. The College Gaudy (a regular event for older members) was introduced in 1990.

The range of clubs included many sports, from athletics to horse riding and windsurfing. The College's punts were stored next to the harbour. In some years the standard of rowing excelled; Margaret launched a new women's eight boat, *The Sir Raymond Hoffenberg*, which regrettably later perished in the Oxford University Boatshed fire. There was a good relationship between Wolfson College and its sister College, Darwin, at Cambridge, that was reflected in an annual sporting and dining event; Hoffenberg represented Wolfson at tennis. He often played tennis with his younger friend, Richard Harries, Bishop of Oxford. Fellows sometimes teased Harries, enquiring solicitously about the outcome of the game, knowing that Hoffenberg almost invariably won.[10]

Some of the Wolfson students' political interest focused on the inequity suffered by the peoples of the developing countries and on race relations in South Africa. The charity to which the College community gave its greatest support was the African Medical and Research Foundation which, unlike many charities, was known to deliver a high proportion of its funds directly to needy recipients. Derek Wyatt chaired a College working party which carried out a serious study of UK companies having South African interests and considered, in particular, industrial relations, migrant labour, pay and wage structure, and desegregation. The outcome of this study influenced the pattern of College investments, and in 1986 Hoffenberg was able to reassure the College that no shares were held in its name in companies which had more than five per cent of their capital employed in South Africa. He was instructed by a General Meeting to seek the withdrawal of the College account with Barclays Bank unless it left South Africa where at the time it was known to have substantial interests. He visited F.R. Goodenough, a Barclays executive (and later Supernumerary Fellow and Honorary Fellow), who replied cautiously; but in fact Barclays had already decided to close their South African operation.[11]

The Senior Tutor and the Tutor for Admissions had direct responsibility for student management but Hoffenberg also took a keen interest in student welfare. In 1986 he wrote:

Five years at medical school tends to produce students in a common mould, fashioned perhaps in the image of their teachers who, one must admit, exhibit a degree of conformity. Students at Wolfson do seem different ... I've enjoyed the enthusiasm most display about their subjects, the excitement that comes from moving into a new and unexpected territory, which contrasts with the rather earnest absorption of medical students obliged to learn too many facts with all-too-rare exposure to the challenge and excitement of modern day biological research.[12]

Over the years there were many debates about how the mentoring of students might be improved. Sometimes it was difficult to find a Fellow with an appropriate academic specialty to mentor a particular student, but individual College Advisers were appointed. In Trinity Term, Hoffenberg and the Senior Tutor would meet all first-year students individually to review their research and study programmes and to discuss future plans – a process known as 'Collections'. Many students, especially those from overseas, suffered social dislocation, and the psychiatrist, Dennis Gath, was often called in to assist. On one occasion Hoffenberg counselled a Chinese student in full flight, popping tranquilizers into his open mouth until he became more quiescent; there were advantages in having a physician as President. However, despite such individual setbacks, the academic performance of Wolfson students, as reflected in the rate of completion of degrees, ranked highly.[13]

Although Hoffenberg experienced few disciplinary problems with students, two particular instances stayed in his memory. On one occasion he had to confiscate a gun from a student about to face his DPhil examination, who was threatening women. About three years later the student returned: 'Do you remember me, President?' He asked for his gun back, and Hoffenberg returned it after assurances of good conduct.[14]

The eviction of another student, Brian Sharpe, from College became a *cause célèbre*. Sharpe was a mature chemistry student who had been taken in under the generous tutelage of Ken Cranstoun. After five years of failing to submit work – Sharpe claiming College burglaries were the cause – the Chemistry Department discontinued his enrolment. Sharpe was given notice to quit the College; he appealed to the College Visitor, but Lord Wilberforce declared the matter 'outside his remit'. The Domestic Bursar, Cecilia Dick, to whom Hoffenberg attributed a mischievous streak, suggested to the Bursar, C.H. Walton, that in Sharpe's absence he might change the lock on his room and remove his belongings to a safe place.

Since no eviction order had been granted, the Oxford City Council intervened, and 'the magistrates fined Wolfson College's President and its Fellows £250 with £157 costs and its Bursar £100 for illegally evicting a student'. Hoffenberg 'called for legal changes to exempt universities and residential colleges from rules protecting tenants', the *Daily Telegraph* carried an editorial supporting Wolfson and a correspondent in *The Times* referred to the long delay associated with enforcing an eviction order.

Margaret and Bill with Adelaide Tambo (*far right*), wife of Oliver Tambo, President of the ANC, and a friend.

Archbishop and Mrs Desmond Tutu, with Bill and Margaret, following an *Encaenia* ceremony at which the Archbishop received an honorary degree from Wolfson College, 1990.

However this was not the end of the matter; Sharpe sued the College and proved, over more than twelve years, to be a vexatious litigant, often failing to appear in court, and so dragging out the proceedings interminably. He rejected a College *ex gratia* payment offer and after he had lost his final appeal, which granted the College costs (which were never paid), Wolfson was many tens of thousands of pounds out of pocket. It was only Sharpe's death which removed this recurring item from the Governing Body agenda.[15]

Hoffenberg sought to increase the rigour of intellectual activity at Wolfson, believing that some fellows treated it as a convenient luncheon club. The annual Wolfson Lecture Series, held in Hilary Term, was the flagship event of the College which culminated in a publication based on the lectures. In 1987, Hoffenberg gave a synoptic lecture 'Modern Medicine: Prospects and Problems' in the series *New Prospects for Medicine*, which Jonathan Austyn edited.[16] Hoffenberg chaired a Working Party on the 'College Vision' which sought to integrate Visiting Scholars better into the life of the College and to stimulate academic exchange between fellows and graduate students through informal association within broad subject groups. New fellows were to be encouraged to give lectures on their area of interest, and a small College fund was created to further their research. In 1987 an appeal was launched to establish an Isaiah Berlin Fellowship in the History of Ideas and in 1989 a lecture fund was established to commemorate the historian and classicist Sir Ronald Syme OM who had been a fellow of Wolfson College for almost 20 years.[17]

The lecture programme for 1991, the 25th anniversary of the College's foundation, demonstrates Hoffenberg's success in broadening the spectrum of academic disciplines at that time. Donald Broadbent convened a series on 'The Simulation of Human Intelligence'. Stephen Jay Gould, from Harvard, delivered the Isaiah Berlin lecture to an overflow audience: 'Making Sense of the Unpredictable: The Role of History and Contingency in Science', whilst the inaugural Syme lecture by Géza Alföldy from Heidelberg was entitled 'Two *Principes*: Augustus and Sir Ronald Syme'. Ken Burras spoke on 'The Evolution of the English Garden' whilst the geologist Jim Kennedy expounded 'Oxford Before Man'. There were also public lectures by Visiting Scholars and a talk preceding each Governing Body meeting. In June a seminar was organized on 'Higher Education: Towards the 21st Century': amongst the participants were Lord Joseph, Baroness Warnock and John Brademas of New York University, and Sir Claus Moser who spoke at the dinner. This eclectic programme supported by so many distinguished speakers indicated that Wolfson now played a significant role in Oxford life.

Another aspect of Wolfson's development was its growth as a centre of contemporary art. This owed much to Margaret Hoffenberg's initiatives and connections. During the Hoffenberg presidency the College acquired or received on long loan many distinguished sculptures and paintings. From 1988 Sir Anthony Caro's exciting bronze, *Double Half,* graced the

Marble Hall,[18] and a Robinson appeared on the verandah of the Upper Common Room. The Arts Subcommittee was given an annual subvention to purchase works and Margaret's friendship with Mr and Mrs Eugene Rosenberg in London led to the loan of eleven pictures, a sculpture and the gift of a Guerrier patchwork quilt. Mrs Janet Wolfson de Botton lent a collection of works, and Bridget Riley, a major representative of Op Art, lent a large painting for the Marble Hall. As Chair of the Arts Subcommittee, Margaret reported in 1989 'we are gaining a reputation in Oxford as a place in which to view innovative, interesting contemporary art'. In 1990 she organized a succession of eight three-week exhibitions, a pattern repeated in later years.[19] The 25-year College Anniversary was celebrated with an art competition; there was a noticeable trend to abstract art in the 503 entries. Steven Tanza's painting *Control*, for which he received £2,500, was hung in the upper part of the marble lobby. Margaret also commenced an internal loan scheme for students. The Wolfson collection became truly international with many African, European and some Asian works.[20]

The Nolte affair

The greatest upheaval that occurred during the Hoffenberg presidency, and which caused real hurt to the Hoffenbergs, concerned an invitation to Professor Ernst Nolte, an historian from Berlin to deliver a lecture. The tumultuous events that followed had their genesis at a meeting of the Academic Planning Committee on 9 March 1988. It was considering potential topics for the 1989 Wolfson lecture series and finally adopted the proposal of Mark Almond, a junior research fellow, on the subject 'Revolution and Counter-Revolution'. At its subsequent gathering on 23 May a tentative list of fifteen potential speakers for eight lectures, which included Nolte, was agreed by majority vote. The usual procedure was for the convenor 'to make tentative enquiries of possible lecturers, usually by telephone', and for the President to issue invitations once the final list of six to eight was agreed.[21]

Almond wrote to Nolte on 10 June, inviting him to lecture in the series; Almond stated he had been told that the Governing Body had approved the speakers, but in fact the Governing Body did not meet until 15 June and did not then consider the matter. Nolte indicated his willingness to lecture, but wrote: 'You presumably know that I have been attacked often and with great sharpness in connection with the so-called *Historikerstreit* [Historians' dispute] … I was invited … in Toronto … but the invitation was withdrawn with the explanation that protests were to be expected.'[22]

Historicism in Germany after World War II underwent many vicissitudes. In the 1970s some left wing historians believed recent German national history represented an aberration [*ein deutscher Sonderweg*] from the norms of liberal western Europe, but more recently there was a counter-movement from the right to legitimate political conditions and to return to the old role of historians in normalizing (i.e. sanitizing) German history by providing a more positive re-evaluation of the Nazi regime, 'which finds its best expression in the writings of Ernst Nolte ... In Nolte's work, Nazism attains historical greatness, and even the dimensions of tragedy, and its murderous side becomes a mere "preventive over-reaction" '.[23] These revisionists sought the rebirth of German nationalism by an attempt 'to relativize the National Socialist crimes and to exculpate German history from its darkest years'.

Nolte did not belong to the revisionists such as David Irving who denied the Holocaust; rather he conceded the atrocities of the Nazis and attempted to humanize them.[24] Nolte stated that: 'The annihilation of several million European Jews, many Slavs, the mentally insane and gypsies is without precedent in its motivation and execution.'[25] He drew parallels with other atrocities: the Armenian massacres in 1915, the Russian Gulag Archipelago, the USA in Vietnam, Pol Pot in Cambodia, and the massacre of communists in Indonesia.[26] These comparisons are methodologically valid, as far as they go, but Nolte's theses were often presented in question form without properly establishing the cause of these events. Stefan Berger suggests that Nolte's overarching interpretation of the history of the twentieth century relied on his 'concept of the "world civil war" between fascism and communism as a variant of the totalitarianist paradigm'.[27]

Nolte believed that the Gulag Archipelago constituted Hitler's model for Auschwitz which, he maintained, did not arise as a result of traditional anti-Semitism but was 'a reaction born out of the anxiety of the annihilating occurrences of the Russian revolution';[28] it was a response to the Bolshevist menace. It is difficult to establish evidence for a causal nexus between the liquidation of kulaks and Hitler's view of the Jews, but Nolte believed it fitted Hitler's psychopathological compulsions. Nolte also believed that 'Chaim Weizmann's declaration at the Zionist World Congress of 1939, that Jews all over the world would fight on Britain's side against Germany, might have been justification enough for the Nazis to intern all German Jews as prisoners of war'.[29]

Nolte's views were a cause of considerable concern to those Wolfson fellows whose family members had been murdered in the Holocaust. The philosopher Raymond Klibansky, a vigorous personality who had fled Heidelberg from the Nazis in 1933,[30] suggested to Hoffenberg that Nolte would be unwelcome at Wolfson. Hoffenberg brought the matter to the

General Purposes Committee on 22 July 1988, which strongly supported the following minute:

> The General Purposes Committee has carefully considered the invitation to Professor Nolte … Whatever decision we take is likely to be wrong in the eyes of some people, on the grounds either that we are transgressing accepted rules of academic freedom or alternatively causing hurt and bitterness to a section of the community. It is likely that a visit by Nolte would provoke large-scale protest and there would always be people within the College whose objections to him would not be overcome by rational persuasion. With some reluctance the GPC therefore decided to take the line that would cause least harm, i.e. to 'disinvite' Nolte.

Hoffenberg told Almond he would be happy to write to Nolte personally to explain the position, but Almond wrote directly to Nolte and also resigned his convenership of the lecture series,[31] which Ellen Rice then agreed to manage.

At a College General Meeting on 19 October Andrew Moore, a graduate student, raised the issue of the conduct of the lecture series, and Hoffenberg expounded the reasons for the decision of the General Purposes Committee, the offence which might be given to those who had suffered at the hands of the Nazis, and the agreed method by which invitations were issued by the President to participants in the lecture series. There was at some stage a leak to the press, and the issue of Nolte speaking at Oxford became a *cause célèbre*.

In the *Sunday Telegraph* of 23 October 1988 Peter Millar reviled Wolfson College for its departure from the norms of academic freedom, and quoted Almond's reference to 'Sir Raymond's connections with the Nobel prize-winning International Physicians against Nuclear War Group, regarded by many Western politicians as a product of the Soviet Propaganda Machine'. This was a group started in 1980 by the American academic, Professor Bernard Lown with Professor Yevgeny Chazov, who became Soviet Minister for Health; in 1985 Hoffenberg was photographed with the Nobel Laureate, Lown, but Hoffenberg had only met Chazov once, at a large dinner in London. This was sufficient for sections of the press to regard Hoffenberg as a crypto-communist and Christopher Booker described him as 'a South African endocrinologist fossilised in an old fashioned left-wing view of the world'.[32] In *The Observer* Richard Ingrams suggested 'a rather cranky but perfectly respectable German Professor has been banned from giving a lecture on the Holocaust for fear of offending the Jewish lobby'; the question of the possible withdrawal of philanthropic support for Wolfson College also arose, at Almond's suggestion. Angela Lambert mistakenly stated in *The Independent* that the Wolfson Governing Body had approved Nolte's invitation at the beginning of June, and

Professor Norman Stone, Almond's mentor, withdrew from the lecture series, arguing for free speech as a paramount value. Lord Dacre stated: 'Nolte is a learned man and entitled to present his thesis.'[33]

The Hoffenbergs also received a series of letters: '? HOLOCAUST ? ALL GAS, NO CHAMBER!' and invitations were issued for a spurious reception at the Pitt-Rivers Museum at which Hoffenberg would present a stuffed werewolf. To add insult to injury three professors from other Colleges, including Adam Roberts of Balliol, invited Nolte to lecture in Oxford during the period of the Wolfson series.[34]

Some academics, such as Dr Hans-Georg Schneider, leapt to the defence of the Wolfson decision. Professor Alexander Kennaway was 'dismayed that Oxford University considers that it is worth listening to Nolte's spurious scholasticism,' whilst C.C. Aronsfeld attacked Nolte: 'he seriously suggests that the Nazis would never have exterminated the Jews if it had not been for the Bolsheviks'. Wolfgang Mommsen, President of the West German Historical Association, pointed out that 'the historical roots of Hitler's anti-Semitism are much older than Bolshevism itself.'[35]

Opinion at Wolfson College was divided, although the majority of both fellows and students supported the decision of the General Purposes Committee to disinvite Nolte. The then Senior Tutor, Ken Cranstoun, defended Almond and attempted to mediate, but Hoffenberg was intransigent. Professor Wlodzimierz Brus would have preferred to allow Nolte to lecture but to give him a hard time in the question period; some fellows who agreed with the Committee's decision reversed their view in hindsight, and others like Martin Francis, who wrote to *The Independent* in support of Hoffenberg, were solidly behind him. The Governing Body on 26 October established a subcommittee: W.S. McKerrow, R.J. Roberts, N.J. Allen and J.F. Ashton, which, by 22 votes to 18, was to confine its deliberations to the publication of material in the press, 'the source of the comments, and whether any action needed to be taken.' Almond denied leaking documents to the press and said that he had simply responded honestly to the questioning of reporters. Hoffenberg's fierce interviewing of Almond, early on in the proceedings, may have influenced Almond's action in clamming up at Wolfson; on 7 November he stated to McKerrow that he might have to resort to legal proceedings. Later Hoffenberg approached Lord Goodman for an opinion; Goodman responded with confidence to let Almond sue.[36]

Hoffenberg, battered by the press campaign and disappointed by the College's lack of trenchant support, offered his resignation on 10 November to Martin Francis, Secretary to the Governing Body, who persuaded him to withdraw it. The Governing Body at its meeting on 21 November decided to take no further action and passed a vote considering the matter to be closed. However there was a strongly attended General Meeting on 23 November at which a German student fiercely attacked Hoffenberg. A resolution recommending to the Governing Body 'that the College as a whole should accept responsibility and not blame any particular individual for the events' was lost 14/20, with 11 abstentions. George Peters' and Jim Kennedy's motion recommending that the matter be regarded as closed and expressing sympathy to those who might have been injured during the course of the Nolte affair was carried 21/12, with 12 abstentions. Hoffenberg again resigned, but the subcommittee of former vicegerents waited on him, and persuaded him to soldier on. Roger Booker, the then vicegerent, Chris Walton, Stuart McKerrow and Martin Francis wrote to *The Spectator*, indicating the Governing Body's full support for Hoffenberg, and this was reaffirmed unanimously at its meeting on 18 January 1989.[37]

Over this period Almond had been active in the press, and his article in *The Spectator* which bore the headline 'Witch Hunters Sabotaged' did not endear him to some sections of the College. Later the General Purposes Committee expressed a reservation about Almond's potential future membership of the Common Room; in the event he did not apply, but this issue further divided the College. In February Nolte addressed a packed meeting in Oxford. There were no demonstrations and Nolte focused on the Left versus Right theory of history, which Sir Isaiah Berlin found profoundly boring.[38]

There is an ironic footnote to these events. Lord Alan Bullock, the historian and writer, had proposed Ernst Nolte as a Visiting Fellow to the Fellowship and Membership Committee at Wolfson and Nolte was elected for the Michaelmas 1978 and Hilary 1979 terms. Nolte, however, decided to go to Darwin College, Cambridge. The people at that committee meeting, such as Roger Booker, Ken Cranstoun and Geoff Garton, who were involved in the events surrounding Nolte's disinvitation, apparently had no recollection of the College's previous legitimation of Nolte. However, the extent of this legitimation was limited, since it was only in the 1980s that Nolte became vocal about his more extreme views.[39]

The Nolte affair caused deep hurt to the Hoffenbergs. It must have aroused their memories of vilification under a totalitarian regime in South Africa. For the early part of 1989 they reduced their involvement in the life of the College and it was probably not until after 1990 that the more relaxed ambience which had previously prevailed at Wolfson was restored. The wounds were caused partly by the ambivalent support by a few fellows for Hoffenberg's defence of what had been a committee decision to disinvite Nolte. His deepest disquiet however, came from the unwarranted public attack on his credentials as a liberal. He had assumed these were beyond challenge, since he had run newspapers (subsequently banned) in South Africa in defence of political freedom, and in the UK he had supported causes – often unpopular – that defended the widest view of human rights.[40]

College governance and infrastructure

The Wolfson Governing Body of approximately 60 fellows contained eminent academics. Sir Anthony Epstein, Peter Bryant, Anthony Hoare, Marshall Stoneham and Donald Broadbent were Fellows of the Royal Society. Geza Vermes, Sebastian Brock and Roger Moorey were fellows of the British Academy. Many were professors and knights, and many of the younger fellows, such as Peter Kanowski, later occupied Chairs. During Hoffenberg's term the balance of disciplines of the Governing Body changed from 59 per cent of fellows in the physical and biological sciences in 1985 to 47 per cent in 1993; some six extra posts went to the humanities and social sciences.[41] This may have reflected the desire of the scientists to have more interesting conversationalists at lunch; but more likely it arose from the strong competition from the undergraduate colleges to recruit scientists to mainstream teaching positions, as for example in chemistry. Hoffenberg was disappointed that to some Wolfson was perceived as a Jewish-oriented College even though it employed lecturers in Islamic Archaeology and History; it also supported studies in Persian Literature and an Emeritus Lecturer in Persian.[42]

Hoffenberg was regarded as an excellent chairperson; he managed to draw out fellows' ideas and to develop a consensus fairly rapidly without precluding the expression of dissident views. Governing Body meetings concluded much earlier than in Sir Henry Fisher's day, allowing a longer interval for pre-dinner drinks. But the real advantage of this was that the College could delay the start of the meeting until later in the afternoon at 5.30 pm which was more convenient for fellows with laboratories in town. Wolfson was run by cycles of many committee meetings, over most of which Hoffenberg presided. He said in 1990: 'I make a practice of abstaining on all voting issues in committee and, so far, have not been required to register a casting vote.' This did not, however, prevent members from having the sense that he preferred matters to be dealt with in his way, unless there were good reasons to adopt an alternative. He would act executively on occasions. At the Faculty Board in Birmingham there had been an interminable debate about the installation of condom vending machines, which was resolved in the negative; at Wolfson Hoffenberg, having received a request from a gay student, had the machines installed without discussion, and with no ensuing opposition.

The Viceregents of 1995–2003, N.J. Allen, G.R. Booker, J.M. Argyle, G.H. Peters and W.J. Kennedy were all highly supportive of Hoffenberg, and Allen and Booker had an especial need to deputize for him whilst he held the Royal College of Physicians presidency. Hoffenberg's relations with G.K.L. (Ken) Cranstoun as Senior Tutor were more problematic, and following the Sharpe and Nolte affairs and some criticism of Cranstoun's handling of financial assistance to graduate students which was perceived as sometimes over-generous, Cranstoun in 1989 resigned early. At the time this caused some disquiet in the College[43] but the quietly indefatigable John Penney became Senior Tutor. Geoff Garton was the part-time Bursar until 1987, when Hoffenberg convinced the College a full-time Bursar with financial skills was needed. There were 166 applications; probably C.H. Walton's experience in Africa and as a divisional executive of the World Bank gave him the inside running with Hoffenberg, and thereafter the College's finances were reorganized to considerable advantage. He was fortunate in his succession of élite personal secretaries: Violet Gray, Ann Cowell, who followed him from the Royal College of Physicians in 1990,

Friends at Bill's 70th birthday luncheon at the President's Lodgings, Wolfson College. *(Left to right)* Margaret Marshall, 1st woman President of the National Union of South African Students (NUSAS), Richard Kershaw, Margaret Hoffenberg, Lady Bannister, Hon. Robert Loder, 1993.

and Sue Hales. He kept an open office door. On occasions he could exhibit hauteur: Stan Woodell once said to Sue Hales: 'Is he in?, provoking a stentorian voice from the inner sanctum: 'Who is *he*?'[44] Hoffenberg cultivated Peter Wallen as chef. On a daily basis the College enjoyed a range of English dishes alongside food from other cultures and the Thursday Guest Nights maintained a high standard.

The Hoffenbergs took a keen interest in the College garden, and were delighted when it gained an Award of Merit from the Royal Horticultural Society; 300 people visited the garden at an Open Day on 28 May 1990. Walter Sawyer made a number of innovations, including the creation of a bog garden by the river. Floodlighting the island to the east of the College harbour was Margaret Hoffenberg's idea; she was also responsible for the attractive refurbishment of the College chairs.[45]

The evolution of the College infrastructure presented many challenges. At the time of Hoffenberg's arrival negotiations were in progress for the College to develop a Science Park at Yarnton on the site of the previous Weed Research Organization. Hoffenberg wrote:

> More than ever before there is a need for closer cooperation between academic and industrial interests, and Wolfson College is especially well-endowed to play a major catalytic role ... A way to 'protect' non-scientific interests at Wolfson would be to divert some of the anticipated income from the proposed Science Park towards the creation of fellowships in the humanities ...[46]

These hopes proved abortive when it became clear that the P&O Company with whom Wolfson were tentatively engaged was using the College's name for their own purposes without proper consultation and would eventually sell their interest.[47]

The second proposal for a Wolfson Science Park was for a site adjacent to the Oxford Railway Station, and negotiations commenced with British Rail and the Carroll Group of Companies as joint developer. By March 1989 it was clear the plan had failed; in hindsight Walton declared that the College lacked the necessary money, expertise and land to develop its own Science Park and organic growth was a preferred option. Nevertheless, Wolfson maintained its policy of seeking industry support for research fellowships linked to company interests.[48]

Wolfson increased the computer facilities for students, and there were two notable and successful expansions of the library, which initially had been intended to reflect 'the library of a good country house'. As the College received bequests of serious collections, such as the Zaehner collection on Indology and comparative religion and the classics library of Sir Ronald Syme, it became necessary to find more space to accommodate them. In 1987 the Hornik Room was created out of a former telephone exchange to house a collection of books concerned predominantly with European intellectual history and art. In 1993, following a gift of £400,000 from Dr Stephen Floersheimer and some other donations, the ground floor beneath the library, formerly occupied by guest rooms and a little-used common room, was taken over to provide mobile stacks and a reading room.[49]

The development of Chinese Studies preoccupied Hoffenberg and the College during 1990 to 1992. Under Henry Fisher there had been a long standing paper association with St Antony's College to study the language and culture of China; Sir John Addis was active in fundraising and Glen Dudbridge, a Wolfson Fellow, was University Lecturer in Chinese. In 1986 it was proposed to establish an Institute of Chinese Studies with its own premises at Wolfson and in 1988 Sir Richard Evans, who had just retired as UK Ambassador to China, was appointed a Senior Research Fellow at the College. Some fellows on the Governing Body were nervous about developing the Institute at Wolfson since, on the one hand, there was a preferred principle of integrating growth within the teaching departments of the University and, on the other, the creation of the Institute might lead to a disciplinary imbalance at Wolfson. Then a certain euphoria developed in March 1990 when it was announced that the Hong Kong magnate Sir Run Run Shaw would give £10 million to the University to establish the Run Run Shaw Institute for Chinese Studies, directed to 'contemporary aspects of the Chinese world, such as politics, economics, finance, trade and sociology'. Sir Richard Southwood, University of Oxford Vice Chancellor, declared it would become 'the intellectual *entrepôt* for the Chinese World and Western Europe'.[50]

The proposal met opposition from local residents. The original site suggested had been 14 Chadlington Road, and Hoffenberg attended a meeting in nearby St Andrews' Church Hall in Linton Road called to discuss the venture. One speaker stated that he had served his country in the defence forces and the last thing he 'wanted was to see a lot of squint-eyed yellow people in this area'. These sentiments were applauded and Hoffenberg intervened to deplore the disgraceful racism expressed. Oxford City Council rejected Wolfson's application, but an alternative site, 33 Linton Road at the north-western entrance to the College, was eventually approved and by December 1991 the old house on the site was being demolished. The Oxford Architects Partnership was commissioned to design the Institute, and produced plans for an elegant three-storey building with a courtyard and colonnade, whose overall design was compatible with the existing College. In June 1992 the Governing Body approved a heads of agreement with the University concerning the management of the Institute and an attractive brochure was printed.[51]

Hoffenberg was to visit Hong Kong in August 1992 as an external examiner. He had issued invitations for a grand dinner there and planned to celebrate Wolfson's new venture in Chinese Studies and to appeal for further funds for the Institute. Four days before departure he learnt in confidence that Sir Run Run Shaw had decided to reduce his gift from £10 million to £3 million in order to 'direct much needed funds to other more urgent causes such as the damage caused by the recent floods in eastern China'; he was also dissatisfied with 'the slow progress of the Institute'. Hoffenberg sought the advice of Chris Patten, Governor of Hong Kong, who suggested not cancelling the dinner. The Hoffenbergs were then obliged to go through the elaborate charade of pretending that this great venture was about to commence, knowing that in fact the Institute would not be built, a truly humiliating experience.

More bad news was to follow. Wolfson had been allocated the Chair of Modern Chinese Studies as part of the residual £3 million donation. However, with the intervention of Glen Dudbridge, who had by now become Professor of Chinese and moved to another college, the funds were diverted to secure two lectureships in the Chinese Department of the Oriental Faculty. The Department became housed in a building previously occupied by the Clarendon Press and Dudbridge's own existing Chair was re-named for Shaw. Hoffenberg attempted to resign from the management committee of the Centre, but was told his position was *ex officio*. A letter was sent to the Secretary of the Faculties of the University:

> The College deplores the decision to dispense with the Chair of Modern Chinese Studies that had been allocated to it. For about 12 years the College has been associated, through the Modern Chinese Studies Centre, with the policy to enhance teaching and research in this important area … The College feels it has been placed in an embarrassing position following the President's visit to Hong Kong in August 1992. He was already aware of Sir Run Run Shaw's decision not to fund the Institute building, but, at meetings with leading academics and industrialists, he spoke enthusiastically about the new Chair in Modern Chinese Studies that had been allocated to Wolfson College and of the role the College would play in this field. The College hopes that the new proposals have been put to Sir Run Run in full and that it has been made clear that the change was not initiated by the College … We are concerned about the potential devaluation of the Centre's activities under the new arrangements.[52]

The College was recompensed for its expenditure and the only residual gain was Oxford City Council's approval for the future redevelopment of 33 Linton Road – now razed to the ground.

Over the years Hoffenberg devoted considerable energy to fundraising for the College; in this respect his success was greater than or equal to that of other Presidents. In 1987 a College Appeal office was set up, and the global network of ex-Wolfsonian local chapters was strengthened. Hoffenberg cultivated his many extra-mural contacts to solicit help for Wolfson and invited them to College social functions. A few fellows considered that some of the Honorary Fellowships or Memberships of the Common Room that had been granted had not met their expectations of the philanthropic tariff; they were however gratified when Hoffenberg, having encouraged the interest of Lord (Leonard) Wolfson, persuaded the Wolfson Foundation to increase its donation towards the proposed new accommodation building from £300,000 to £800,000.[53]

This accommodation building, sited in the northern precinct near the squash courts, represented in one sense the culmination of the Hoffenberg presidency. The Oxford Architects Partnership was again commissioned, and produced a graceful two-storey building with a central courtyard, housing students in sets of three or four rooms, each with kitchen and bathroom facilities. Donations were drawn from a wide net to meet the forecast cost of £1.8 million and the building was eventually named after Robin Gandy, a generous benefactor and a former Reader in Mathematical Logic who had been associated with the College from 1970 until his death in 1995. The Bursar, C.H. Walton developed a clever project which took advantage of the Conservative Government's Business Expansion Scheme. By selling the building to public investors and buying it back later, the College was able to gain about £300,000 from the tax allowances this arrangement offered. Before the Scheme was discontinued Walton was able to implement a second buy-back project which temporarily sold 97 study-bedrooms and four flats for a gain of £900,000. Hoffenberg was especially delighted by the completion of the Gandy Building in 1993, since it meant that more students would be able to live in College in their second year.[54]

Vale Wolfson

During his eight years at Wolfson, Hoffenberg did not take a significant role in Oxford University politics; his place was in a wider society. Advised by W.J. Kennedy he initiated meetings with the other heads of postgraduate colleges with the object of reducing the gap between the disadvantaged salary status of their fellows relative to that of fellows of undergraduate colleges. In later years the gap was reduced, but the postgraduate colleges could never match the emoluments linked to housing and other fringe benefits offered elsewhere in Oxford. In 1989 Hoffenberg assumed the Chair of the University Committee for Disabled People, which then met in the President's Rooms. The Committee's work resulted in considerable modifications to access to university premises and in the provision of other services to the handicapped.[55] Apart from these activities, his Oxford focus remained Wolfson College.

Hoffenberg delivered his valedictory lecture at Wolfson in June 1993 on the subject of medical ethics – in particular end of life issues. He took his title from the James Bond film 'Live and Let Die'.[56] A portrait was commissioned from Allan Ramsay; this hangs in the College Library and has met with almost universal disapprobation. To encourage more out-door events, he donated a South African style barbecue to the College which was placed near the tennis courts in the northeast precinct. The College gave the Hoffenbergs carafes, decanters and other drinking accoutrements by the superb silversmith Robert Welsh of Chipping Camden. There was a barbecue send-off – marred by rainy weather – complete with brass band and fireworks over the river, and a Valedictory Dinner. Hoffenberg departed in September 1993 as an Honorary Fellow, whilst Margaret became an Honorary Member of Common Room.[57]

Inevitably, Hoffenberg's presidency of Wolfson attracted a few dissenters, but the greater part of the College community valued him immensely – not least for the compassion he showed towards his colleagues.

One fellow recounted confiding in him about a personal professional disappointment; Hoffenberg responded humbly: 'Oh Julian, if you knew how many failed applications there have been in my life.' To Roger Booker he exhibited 'the physique and bearing which contributed to a natural authority which he combined with charisma and lucid exposi-tion'. To Jon Stallworthy he was 'a lovely man, wise, considerate and courteous'. In the latter part of his term Hoffenberg wrote about his perception of the College:

> We have established a graduate society of a character and importance unique to Oxford, if not to Britain. Students come to us because they value the emphasis we place on their welfare, both academic and social; overseas visitors come because they are encouraged to join in all our activities, as individuals or as families, and to feel part of the College. Everyone appreciates the friend-liness and helpfulness of our staff. In all of these respects, and despite our con-siderable growth over the years, we have managed to retain the collegiate spirit that was so much a part of our existence in the Banbury Road days.[58]

CHAPTER EIGHT

Maintaining standards of medical practice

The Royal College of Physicians

In 1518 the physician and scholar, Thomas Linacre, sought a charter from Henry VIII to control standards of medical practice in the City of London. This led to the formation of the Royal College of Physicians, which continues to this day its principal endeavour to improve and maintain standards of practice in medicine. Since its foundation the College has had five homes. The modern College, located among the 19th century Nash terraces of Regent's Park, was designed by the modernist architect Sir Denys Lasdun and opened in 1964. It is considered one of London's finest 20th century buildings. The main part of the College – comprising lecture theatres, libraries, meeting and reception rooms – is set on three floors around a large atrium with a central staircase designed to give added drama to ceremonial occasions. At the foot of the staircase is the Censors' room, its walls lined with 17th century Spanish oak paneling that had previously graced the walls of two of the earlier college buildings. This room, which in the earlier colleges was used to conduct examinations, now serves as a robing room for College Officers and a starting point for ceremonial processions. It is also brought into service as an elegant private dining room. Another wing houses offices which overlook the College garden. This wing adjoins a Georgian precinct comprising two impressive tall stuccoed houses and an elegant terrace of eight smaller four storey houses, now converted for College use.

On one side of the atrium is the magnificent galleried Dorchester Library, so called because it houses the Marquis of Dorchester's valuable collection of more than 3,000 books. He bequeathed the collection to the College on his death in 1680, the original College library having been lost in the Great Fire of London. On one wall hangs a large portrait of William Harvey (1578–1657), physician and scientist who first described and demonstrated the circulation of the blood. In an indenture dated 1656 Harvey exhorted:

> …the Fellows and members of the College to search out and study the secrets of nature by way of experiment; and also for the honour of the profession, to

continue in mutual love and affection amongst themselves, without which neither the dignity of the College can be preserved, nor yet particular men receive that benefit by their admission into the College which else they might expect...[1]

It is in the Dorchester library that many formal College occasions take place – such as the Membership and Fellowship ceremonies and Comitia – and where until recently the presidential elections were held.

The Royal College of Physicians and (*below*) its precinct.

Election to the presidency

Hoffenberg had become a Fellow of the College in 1971, an Examiner in 1974, a Censor in 1978 and was elevated to Senior Censor (Vice President) in 1981. Following Sir Douglas Black's decision to resign the presidency on taking up a senior official appointment, the election for a successor was held in March 1983. The traditional method of election required that Fellows attend the College in person to cast a vote at a *Comitia* (named after the Roman assembly which elected magistrates and legislated). This ancient attendance requirement (since abolished) almost disfranchised physicians who had no easy access to London. Regional physicians there-fore began to organize fleets of buses to bring them to London to support their favoured candidate – and provide a day's outing to London. Election day thus became a more intense and festive occasion.

Hoffenberg's colleagues in Birmingham, where he was then Professor of Medicine, had persuaded him to accept nomination and stand for elec-tion to the Presidency. His friend, George Whitfield, a physician and Director of Postgraduate Medical Education at Birmingham, sent out over 400 hand-written letters of support to potential voters and on the day of the election many Fellows from the West Midlands duly took their places in the College.[2]

Queen Elizabeth II about to sign the Visitors' Book in the Censors' Room at the College before the opening the St Andrews Place precinct, 11 June 1986.

There was a buzz of excitement in the Library on 28th March with 24 candidates facing the electorate. As tradition dictated, votes were placed in silver rose bowls, individually opened and read out – while Fellows discreetly placed their bets on the likely outcome. On the first ballot Hoffenberg received 249 votes (nearly 100 were from Midland supporters) and Professor Dame Sheila Sherlock, the distinguished hepatologist, received 164. A further ballot was held between the two leading contenders, Hoffenberg winning by 526 votes to Sheila Sherlock's 273. Greatly disappointed by the result, she declaimed within hearing: 'to think that I brought him to this country!' This was not entirely true since Hoffenberg's first post in England was with the Medical Research Council at Mill Hill. He does however appear to have been the first President of the College not to have been born in Britain.

Hoffenberg watched the afternoon's proceedings from the gallery. After the result was announced he joined the Fellows in the body of the library. There he was gowned and handed the *caduceus* (the silver cane of office presented to the College in 1556 by its then President, Dr John Caius). He was formally admitted to the Office of President by the Senior Censor. His first duty as President was to recite 'I dissolve Comitia'; at dinner later that evening he was to make a longer speech. David Pyke, the College Registrar, sought to allay Hoffenberg's nervousness by walking him briskly round Regent's Park – the first of many acts of friendship that marked their collaboration.[3]

In an important respect this election was the culmination of Hoffenberg's professional career; it now fell to him to speak publicly for medicine. He was inundated with congratulatory messages: in his family papers there are 431 from 21 countries, indicating the great constituency of friends and medical colleagues, institutions and professional bodies that he had amassed. He was addressed as 'Bill, Billy, William, Raymond, Dr, Professor' and from the sculptor Rosie Sturgess, 'Bill you old darling'. Spike Spilkin, an ex-captain of the University of Cape Town Golf Club, cabled: 'Wonderful news hope golf and booze not affected.'

Professor M. Gelfand wrote: 'I often think of that small enclave of Groote Schuur, with the mountain towering above it, where we first received the inspiration to practise good medicine.' The South African press reclaimed Hoffenberg as their own. The *Weekend Argus* reported:

> Professor Raymond Hoffenberg's appointment as President of the Royal College of Physicians is very 'challenging and exciting' – but nothing will ever compensate him for his enforced exile from South Africa. He said: 'It is 15 years to the day that I arrived in England ... and I am extremely resentful – not just for myself, but for the thousands like me who have suffered by the wicked abuse of a powerful law to ban anyone without recourse to a court of law ... I cannot

claim that it has done my career any harm. But it still makes me extremely angry to think that some narrow-minded bigot could decide my future like that. South Africa was my country too. I was born there and I had as much right to live there as [then Prime Minister] Vorster or any of those people who decided to ban me. I would much rather have stayed.' Professor Peter Folb said: 'We did not only lose Bill Hoffenberg ... we lost numerous other people as a consequence – people who left of their own accord, who felt they could not tolerate that intrusion on the medical and scientific community ... He told us officially there was nothing he knew that he had done against the law of the land.'[4]

College life

The Royal College of Physicians plays a leading role in the delivery of high quality patient care by setting standards of medical practice and promoting clinical excellence. It provides physicians in the United Kingdon and overseas with education, training and support throughout their careers. It advises the Government, the public and the profession on healthcare and medical matters.

In Britain a physician is a doctor who has undergone specialist training in physic (medicine) as opposed to surgery. Membership of one of the three Royal Colleges of Physicians (London, Edinburgh or Glasgow) is a prized professional qualification achieved through examination; gaining MRCP(UK) is the usual first step *en route* to becoming a consultant physician.

The presidents of the College are given a fairly free rein in setting its agenda. Identification of pressing healthcare issues on which the College chooses to focus and move forward is strongly influenced by the President – working in close collaboration with the College Officers. Fellows and Members delivering healthcare in hospitals in the regions also highlight their concerns arising from their day-to-day practice. Education, training and workforce issues account for a great deal of presidential time. The President is required to respond to significant events as they happen and to represent the profession in dealings with the government. The College supported and was closely involved in the creation of the NHS in 1948 and has remained committed to its first principle, that healthcare is available free of charge at the point of need.

Hoffenberg found his fellow officers to be congenial and, in the main, supportive. He developed an especially close working – and sparring – relationship with the Registrar, David Pyke and the pair continuously enlivened College meetings. Pyke, who was well known for his acerbic humour, wrote:

In the seating arrangements at committees I am always put next to the President – so that I can prompt him or he me; the first is not needed, the second not effective ... The Treasurer [Tony Dawson] and I agree with the President about (practically) everything. But he has noticed a physical sign of dissent in us – when the Treasurer calls him 'President' or I call him 'Sir' he knows there will be trouble. The alternative is dumb insolence ... The President was offered by some enterprising merchant the car number RCP1. The news started a row among the Officers. Who would have RCP2? Fortunately the President declined.[5]

Hoffenberg relied heavily on Stephanie Hall, the Press and Public Relations Adviser, to bring the College's policies and activities to the attention of the Press and media, and on Ann Cowell, who moved from Birmingham to London as his secretary, for the smooth running of his office and organization of his very busy schedule. A private flat is provided within the College building for the President's use. This gave the Hoffenbergs a base in London. Dinner jackets had to be kept ready both in London and Birmingham (and later also at Oxford), since Hoffenberg had to juggle so many formal engagements in his dual roles. Michael Tibbs was the ever diplomatic College Secretary, who had stepped a careful path during 18 years of negotiation between the local Camden Council, responsible for planning regulations, and the Crown Commissioners, who owned the leasehold, in the acquisition of ten Georgian houses in the St Andrews Place precinct, and their conversion for College use.

Hoffenberg was knighted KBE by the Queen in June 1984 for services to medicine. Earlier when he and Margaret were invited to stay at Windsor Castle he was commissioned to advise the Queen that her long arranged visit to the College to open the building in the precinct should be delayed because 'dry rot' had been found there. The delayed opening eventually took place on a sunny day on 11 June 1986. The acquisition of The Precinct – as it is always known – greatly expanded both the educational, administrative and residential facilities of the College. A new state-of-the-art educational facility has since been built on at the rear. Bernard Lloyd, who succeeded Tibbs, found Hoffenberg to be a workaholic, but also a laidback, natural administrator with considerable presence and physical stature who, when necessary, could scale the high locked doors of the back entrance to the College car park with ease if the front entrance was locked. His friend, Robert Mahler, at that time a consultant at Northwick Park hospital – and, incidentally, great nephew of Gustav – was appointed Editor of the College journal; Hoffenberg gave him complete editorial freedom, but said facetiously: 'You don't need to accept my papers for publication but remember we can fire you.'[6]

Anthony Hopkins, a consultant neurologist at St Bartholomew's hospital was appointed Director of the College's Research Unit. Under him and with the strong support and enthusiasm of Hoffenberg, the unit's

Four presidents of the Royal College of Physicians. *Left to right*: Sir Douglas Black, Sir Lesley Turnberg (then President), Dame Margaret Turner Warwick (Bill's immediate successor and the College's first woman president) and Bill, 1992.

In the Dorchester Library celebrating the retirement of the long serving Secretary of the Royal College of Physicians, Michael Tibbs, pictured with his wife Anne, 1986.

remit changed radically. It became, and remains 'primarily concerned with the systematic evaluation of the quality and effectiveness of medical care, defining outcomes of illness and evaluating the success of medical intervention'.

Membership and Fellowship

Junior hospital doctors who wish to train in a medical specialty and progress in their careers must first gain the diploma of Membership of the Royal College of Physicians (MRCP(UK)). Although the percentage of those who now pass the examination is greater than when Hoffenberg first attempted it in 1952, the standards required to pass remain just as rigorous. The examination tests core medical skills and practical clinical skills; gradually greater emphasis came to be placed on clinical practice and problem solving rather than simply on factual knowledge. That trend continued, wholeheartedly supported by Hoffenberg who had long advocated the merits of hands-on clinical experience in medical training over learning facts by rote. As well as migrating to the regions outside London, the examination began to be held in Hong Kong. It has since extended to other countries, at their request, where attainment of MRCP(UK) is seen to denote the highest standards of medical practice. The examination has also been harmonised with the Scottish Colleges of Physicians in Edinburgh and Glasgow; candidates from all three Colleges now take the same examination.[7]

Fellows were elected to the Royal College of Physicians (FRCP), several years after they gained their Membership, if they exhibited 'standing in a Royal College, academical honours, distinctions and other relevant considerations'. Latterly, the time between gaining Membership and election to the Fellowship has been considerably shortened. Members who are consultant physicians in the NHS (the largest category of nominees) are usually elected to the Fellowship three or four years after being appointed to a consultant post. Having been endorsed at regional level, proposals for Fellowship are scrutinized first by the Registrar, then the President, then by a committee of Council – and finally by Council itself. In reviewing them Hoffenberg looked for some specific contribution to the College, to teaching, or to public affairs, while David Pyke, who also reviewed each nomination, was zealous in ensuring standards of professional integrity were met. Pyke wrote in 1987:

> The day of admission of new Fellows is the highlight of the College year ... One Nobel prizewinner and four Fellows of the Royal Society at the top of the list, more than 20 overseas Fellows coming to London specially for the occasion.[8]

Educating physicians – the College's role

The maintenance of high standards in medical practice depends increasingly on the continuing medical education of practising physicians. In this the College has always played a major role by organizing conferences and lectures, and a programme of 'teach-ins' directed to younger physicians. Latterly, with the introduction of mandatory continuing professional development, it has become a major provider of educational events, courses and online and printed materials. One of Hoffenberg's achievements was to extend the College's activities to the regions outside London. A network of regional advisers was already in place and Hoffenberg built on this by encouraging the appointment of College Tutors in each National Health Service District. These Tutors were tasked to advise and assist junior doctors in their career development and to help guide them in preparing for the MRCP examination; by 1989 almost 200

Presenting a commemorative plaque to Patricia Kincaid-Smith, President of the Royal Australasian College of Physicians at the College's Golden Jubilee Meeting in Sydney, June, 1988.

had been appointed. The College conference, lecture and teach-in programme was also expanded into the regions outside London. Hoffenberg
and Robert Mahler prevailed on the Lilly Drug Company to increase its
subvention for the eponymous Lilly Lecture, so that the College could
draw on speakers from anywhere in the world and so that the lecture
could be delivered at a hospital in the regions as well as in London.[9]

The College's educational programme was enhanced by its close association with its specialist Faculties. These were housed in the Precinct and
included Occupational Medicine, Community Medicine (now Public
Health Medicine) and a new Faculty of Pharmaceutical Medicine which
Hoffenberg had enthusiastically helped to set up. However, the British
Paediatric Association – also housed in the Precinct – which he hoped
would become a faculty under the aegis of the three Royal Colleges of
Physicians, later chose to become a separate College and moved to new
premises. In 1988 the College had 34 scholarships and fellowships in its
gift which were used to support mainly younger physicians who wished
to embark on research or to practice abroad for a period – often in a
developing country – and for College lectureships.[10]

Undergraduate education

The standard and type of teaching in medical schools and the undergraduate curriculum are crucial to the standards of practice achieved later
in a doctor's career. Hoffenberg's strongly held view of the need for reform
was expressed in a lecture he gave in 1993 at the University of Bristol,
where he received an honorary MD. He maintained that the curriculum
should reflect not only the major scientific advances in medicine but
include access to sophisticated technology. He also advocated that, rather
than placing great emphasis on the acquisition of ever burgeoning
amounts of factual knowledge – which he attributed in part to the then
prevailing lack of motivation among students – there should be far more
contact with patients in the pre-clinical years of undergraduate education.
He was clear that good basic science combined with training in clinical
method would provide a sound basis for a medical career, and help to
ensure the adaptability that doctors must exhibit if they wish to keep
abreast of changes that will take place during their professional careers.
Only up-to-date clinical skills could provide the basis for deciding which
of the available technologies would be needed to treat a patient, make a
diagnosis or, importantly, deciding whether they would be needed at all.[11]

He went on to suggest ways in which science could be given more
prominence in clinical medical training. It might be achieved in a direct
way through the BSc or BMedSc intercalated during the course, or the

combination of clinical medicine and subsequent study leading to a PhD or MD: 'All students should learn that medicine is largely a science.' Students should have time to think, to explore what interested them and be encouraged to question what they were taught. He added:

> I was taught to use treatments that no longer exist for diseases that no longer exist: not because they've been eliminated by scientific advance, they didn't exist in the first place! The facts that we are taught today are likely to be superseded by better and more sustainable facts in a doctor's practising lifetime.

An appetite for learning might be encouraged 'based on curiosity and the exploration of knowledge rather than its passive acquisition'; the emphasis should move to self-learning and to problem solving. He also commented: 'Clinician-teachers become the models on which students fashion themselves, and they soon learn to distinguish the good from the bad.'

The teaching of clinical method required exposure to clinical medicine at the bedside, best experienced by 'apprenticeship'. Hoffenberg considered that 'the basic clinical skills of history-taking, physical and psychological examination and communication demand time with individual patients, which is best provided in hospital wards'. He regarded the wards in university hospitals as the most likely to expose students to the latest scientific advances.

Academic medicine

Another of Hoffenberg's major preoccupations was the great importance of academic medicine – the deployment of clinical staff engaged in research. A preliminary working party report was published in September 1987 following which he chaired an 'Academic Medicine Group' comprising doctors from a variety of medical specialties but widened to include university administrators. The group's first report expressed concern at the reduction of clinical teaching posts, the divergence of the basic science from clinical departments, and suggested that the increased number of short-term appointments funded by extra-mural grants could not compensate for the loss of permanent academic staff who undertook long-term basic research. Reductions in the number of senior registrars engaged in research and in the facilities for research and teaching at NHS hospitals had impacted on academic medicine, as had the parsimony of the University Grants Committee. There were also difficulties for doctors who wished to pursue part of their career in research and return to clinical medicine at a later date. All these problems needed to be addressed if the future development of healthcare was to be assured.[12]

Whilst recognizing the important contribution played by the charities that fund research, the Committee identified a discrepancy between the sums received for research into the higher profile conditions, such as heart disease and cancer, and sums received to support research into those conditions that received less public prominence.

The doctor–patient relationship

It was in the area of medical ethics that some of Hoffenberg's colleagues considered he made most impact during his presidency of the Royal College of Physicians. In this he continued and widened the commitment that his predecessor, Sir Douglas Black (then President of the Institute of Medical Ethics) had to these issues.

Since the doctor–patient relationship is fundamental to the delivery of good medical care doctors needed to develop excellent communication skills so as to be able to explain to patients – or their relatives – the purpose and likely outcome of the treatment available to them. Patient autonomy and the obligations and authority of the physician in caring for the patient could sometimes be perceived as being in tension. In his Rock Carling lecture on clinical freedom, Hoffenberg quoted from his friend, the ethicist the Reverend Gordon Dunstan, who had divided patient autonomy into: 1. A patient's right to choose *not* to be treated, and 2. The right to choose a particular treatment. The first notion is relatively clear cut: treatment of competent patients against their wishes constitutes an assault in law, except in emergencies. In the UK, the courts had upheld the right of the patient to refuse treatment on religious grounds, even in life-threatening situations. However, a right of the patient to choose a particular medical treatment raises ethical issues for physicians who Hoffenberg believed were 'not under any obligation to offer treatment or carry out investigations that they consider unnecessary or harmful'.

He was critical of the trend in the USA towards the practice of 'defensive medicine'. Whilst this may reduce a doctor's exposure to litigation (which is far more prevalent in the US health care system than in the UK), in Hoffenberg's view it abandoned the duty of care inherent in the physician's role. The doctor's responsibility was to ensure a genuinely informed consent, bearing in mind the aversion that patients have to invasive procedures that are not essential.[13] He wrote:

> My concern to preserve the central role of the doctor in clinical decisions, moral or otherwise, is not a reflection of self-interest or a wish to perpetuate professional sovereignty. It is based on my belief that such decisions must rest on a proper knowledge of all the medical consequences of each option, physical and psychological, qualitative as well as quantitative; that they must

be made with critical and professional detachment; and that they should be conveyed to and discussed with the patient and the family with compassion and sensitivity.[14]

In a lecture given to the Royal Australian Army Medical Corps in 1994 he recognized that doctors practising in the defence forces or on behalf of commercial companies were acting in a special role, which might raise particular dilemmas. Confidentiality about a patient's condition, paramount in most medical practice, might not always apply. For example, an Army doctor is expected to report malingering and similarly a company insurance doctor is expected to report medical conditions likely to shorten life. The view is that the usual doctor–patient relationship changes in circumstances where the doctor is acting 'as an impersonal technical screening agent'. The relationship is, however, restored when the doctor renders treatment subsequently. Hoffenberg also noted that in some circumstances a moral obligation not to cause harm to others – i.e. when the medical condition of a patient may put others in danger – may override patient confidentiality.[15]

Audit and ethics

During his presidency (1983–1989) Hoffenberg convened and chaired many working parties covering a range of issues particularly salient to medicine at that time and which he judged important to further the College's aims in maintaining and improving medical standards. Medical audit and ethical matters received his greatest attention.

Medical audit

Hoffenberg firmly believed that the best response to public questioning of the standards of medical competence was reform from within the profession. He suggested that scrutiny of medical practice should not be regarded as an encroachment of authority but should be welcomed, for 'only by such scrutiny can we lay any claim to preservation of the clinical freedom we so fortunately enjoy':

> What is needed is less emphasis on the audit of structural or procedural aspects of medical care or on the costs of items of service, more evaluation of personal clinical aspects; less concern with institutions and authorities, more with individual patients and individual doctors ...
> There are doctors who are rude, inconsiderate, unsympathetic, even negligent or venal ... There are also doctors who are ill-informed or ignorant of modern medicine, whose judgement is inadequate, whose use of costly medical techniques in the management of patients is too extravagant or too

parsimonious, who make too many errors that lead to suffering, or, even death … Experience suggests that not many are seriously incompetent, but how do we know how many there are or who they are if we do not look? We should not delude ourselves that our behaviour and competence are always beyond criticism …

Having established with his colleagues systematic medical audit throughout Birmingham hospitals (see Chapter 6)[16] which had proved an effective tool in raising standards of practice, he set up a College working party on the subject which recommended that medical audit should be adopted nationally. The presence of Fellows on audit teams would help to explain the purpose of audit and to monitor its implementation. After initial resistance both by some doctors and by the government, audit came to be regarded as one of the cornerstones of good medical practice within the National Health Service – and indeed in later years became mandatory. Ironically, procedures became considerably more bureaucratic than perhaps Hoffenberg would have envisaged or wished.[17]

Physicians and the pharmaceutical companies

The relationship between doctors and the pharmaceutical companies also concerned Hoffenberg. He recognized that the development and production of new drugs by the pharmaceutical companies was vital to the advancement of medicine, and that there needed to be a close and constructive relationship with the doctors who prescribe them. After prolonged testing in other non-clinical settings, new drugs are evaluated on individual patients. Once they have been carefully assessed and approved for clinical use, the industry, not unnaturally, encourages doctors to prescribe them. It is unethical for doctors to accept gifts or payments as enticements but it was not unknown for financial support to be given to doctors and spouses to attend professional educational meetings – many were held in very attractive locations overseas. The College working party report on these issues had a considerable influence. It suggested that pharmaceutical companies should fund the conference organizers rather than individual delegates, and avoid any promotional activity for a particular product at these meetings. Strict publication standards also needed to be applied to the results of trials. A paper from the International Forum for Transplant Ethics, of which Hoffenberg was a member, acknowledged the role of large pharmaceutical companies in developing more effective drugs. It suggested, however, 'that presentation of data can be delayed, adverse results withheld, and individual investigations hampered. Clinical trials may be protracted to stifle competition. Monetary considerations may transcend common sense'.[18]

Fraud and misconduct in medical research

Internal surveys of the profession suggested that cases of fraud or misconduct were not uncommon. Suspicion might arise, for example, when a scientist produced an inordinate volume of papers, or when a head of department attached his name to his colleagues' research – perhaps generating as many as 200 papers in a year.[19] Stimulated by the concern of Stephen Lock, a Fellow and one time editor of the *British Medical Journal,* Hoffenberg set up a working party on fraud and misconduct in medical research. Three types of misconduct were identified: *piracy* – the exploitation of ideas from others without acknowledgement; *plagiarism* – the copying of ideas without permission or acknowledgement; and *fraud* – which involved deliberate deception and usually the invention of data. Few instances of fraud had been identified, but in an address 'Cooking the Books', Hoffenberg expounded some infamous cases. He cited William McBride's false claim that Debendox caused birth defects. McBride had traded on his significant reputation for having previously uncovered the adverse effects of thalidomide and Hoffenberg suggested that his falsification of data and self-destructive dishonesty fitted the syndrome described by Peter Medawar of the scientist with a 'Messianic complex'.

The working party recommended that allegations of fraud or misconduct should be approached as follows: 1. Decide whether to pursue an inquiry; this might impanel no more than three scientists of distinction to conduct an investigation, bearing in mind the duty to establish truth. 2. Give the respondent the opportunity to defend the work in question. 3. Avoid opportunity for defamation proceedings by maintaining confidentiality. 4. Scientific error will usually be dealt with by the institution itself whereas confirmed findings of scientific misconduct should be referred to the General Medical Council.

Research on healthy volunteers and patients

Hoffenberg also considered that the ethical standards surrounding the participation of patients or healthy volunteers in medical research needed further scrutiny and greater clarity. He set up two further College working parties to develop guidelines for on these issues. The first, *Research on Healthy Volunteers,* emphasized the need for the research to be scientifically and ethically justified and suggested the exclusion of some groups: students who were under the supervision of the scientist conducting the research, children, the elderly, pregnant women, and the mentally handicapped – unless the research topic was particularly pertinent to them. Research using prisoners raised special issues since power-based relationships should not bear on consent. The report also included guidance on informed consent, confidentiality of records, insurance issues and the limits of payment to volunteers participating in research. A second working party, *Research involving Patients*, raised similar issues but gave special attention to the ethical considerations in the use of placebos in clinical trials, and the use of the 'double blind' design where the physician assessing the patient is unaware of whether they were receiving the active compound or a placebo.

The College gave much attention to the composition, establishment and guidance of Local Research Ethics Committees which regulated medical research. *Guidelines for Local Research Ethics Committees Involved in Research on Human Subjects* was first published in 1984 and is now in its 4th edition.[20]

An early attempt at setting standards had been made by a Prussian Minister in 1900:

> Medical intervention for purposes other than diagnosis, therapy and immunization are absolutely prohibited if the person ... has not declared unequivocally that he consents ... and if the declaration has not been made on the basis of a proper exploration of the adverse consequences that may result ...

This initiative in Prussia has a certain irony in view of the subsequent experiments by Nazi doctors, which were carried out in the name of medical investigation but disregarded the sufferings of the victims.

No fault compensation

Medical accidents in the UK, whether arising from a doctor's negligence, untoward side effects of treatment or from simple ill-fortune have attracted rising levels of compensation payments and the insurance premiums paid by doctors. Hoffenberg, remembering the earlier interest of the British Medical Association in 1983 in introducing a scheme for no-fault compensation for medical injury, set up a College working party to pursue this idea further. When considering the increase in defensive medicine in the USA, he contended that: 'the unfairness, the futility, the damaging consequences of the present system of compensating those injured' demanded a new approach, as had been adopted in the no-fault compensation schemes in New Zealand, Sweden and Finland. The adversarial tort system led to inequity for both plaintiff and defendant and was deficient in terms of the delays, costs and quality of representation. Furthermore the large lump sum awards were often inappropriate and were not necessarily used for the purpose for which they were awarded. The differences between medical and legal approaches to the analysis of medical accidents resulted in perverse outcomes.

The New Zealand approach, in which a victim obtained compensation simply by proving injury without attribution of blame, provided a rapid resolution for the victim, and the medical profession took responsibility for dealing with malpractice. The College Report urged:

> A no-fault scheme, limited to compensating the adverse effects of medical intervention, should be introduced with the following features:
> i.   Economic damages recoverable under such a scheme should be capped ...
> ii. Non-economic damages (e.g. pain and suffering) should also be capped.
> iii. Those wishing to avoid any shortfall in their expectations under such a scheme should have recourse to the insurance market ...
> iv. Victims of medical mishaps should be disqualified from suing in negligence if they have already elected to claim under the no-fault compensation scheme ...
> v.   The amounts payable under the no-fault scheme in the form of a lump sum should be strictly limited. Wherever practicable, periodic payments should be made, subject to review at stated intervals.

The working party also proposed procedural rules for medical negligence cases and improvements in court practice for tort actions. These proposals met with fierce opposition from the legal profession and were never implemented. Many years later, however, they are still part of an active agenda in many countries.[21]

The departure

Throughout his six years as President of the College Hoffenberg sought foremost to continue to raise the standards of medical practice. To this end his principal achievements were:

- to influence change in the medical undergraduate and post-graduate curricula, giving more emphasis to communication with patients, as well as to basic science, and clinical method
- to extend College educational activities out into the regions
- with the support of working parties, to shine a light on many of the ethical issues in medicine – clarifying them and providing guidance where none had previously existed.

Hoffenberg was a particularly effective ambassador for the College, travelling widely – which he greatly enjoyed – and forging strong links with many countries which have remained strong and have greatly enhanced the College's influence overseas. With some of the College Officers and Fellows, he attended many overseas conferences – usually organized jointly by the College and the host country. It was usual on these occasions for the Fellowship of the College to be conferred on physicians of high standing who had made a particularly significant contribution to medicine in their country, thus ensuring their continuing association with

The Hoffenberg bust by Elisabeth Frink (by permission of the Frink Estate).

the London College. At a conference in Thailand, in 1988, Queen Sirikit was made an Honorary Fellow in recognition of her work to improve healthcare in that country.

Hoffenberg's departure from the College in 1989 was marked by a grand dinner hosted by the College Officers. He was also invited to a lively afternoon party, organized by the staff, where he was presented with a balloon festooned wheelbarrow – his love of gardening was well known – and there was much mirth when he and Margaret were given bespoke T-shirts emblazoned with 'PRCP 1983–1989'.

Traditionally, the College commissions a portrait of each of its departing presidents, allowing them to choose the artist. For Hoffenberg a bust by Elisabeth Frink, then Britain's most famous living sculptor, was commissioned. In its prominent place in the College it is much admired as an excellent likeness, a fine work of art and a fitting memorial to a distinguished president.

CHAPTER NINE

The delivery of health services

A quarrel with Government

The National Health Service (NHS) is a prime component of the British welfare state, and although many doctors opposed its inception, it came to be regarded as an innovative and successful experiment which delivered good patient care equitably and effectively across all strata of society. By December 1987, when medical services had grown in breadth and sophistication and when the public expectations of access to a wider range of treatment had increased, its resources were inadequate to meet demand. Hoffenberg, then President of the Royal College of Physicians, joined with Ian Todd, President of the Royal College of Surgeons, and George Pinker, President of the Royal College of Obstetricians, to protest about inadequate funding of the NHS. Their statement, published in *The Lancet*, became a *cause célèbre* as the issue was taken up in the media and in Parliament. They wrote:

> Each day we learn of new problems in the NHS – beds are short, operating rooms are not available, emergency wards are closed, essential services are shut down in order to make financial savings. In spite of the efforts of doctors, nurses and other hospital staff, patient care is deteriorating. Acute hospital services have almost reached breaking point. Morale is depressingly low.
>
> It is not only patient care that is suffering. Financial stringencies have hit academic aspects of medicine in particular, because of the additional burden of reduced University Grants Committee funding. Yet, the future of medicine depends on the quality of our clinical teachers and research workers.
>
> Face-saving initiatives such as the allocation of £30 million for waiting lists are not the answer. An immediate overall review of acute hospital services is mandatory. Additional and alternative funding must be found. We call on the Government to do something now to save our Health Service, once the envy of the world.[1]

The paragraph on academic medicine was Hoffenberg's contribution. The protest came at a time when the House of Commons was debating unpopular measures to impose charges for eye tests and dental checks, measures opposed by the British Medical Association. There was a rift in the Conservative Party ranks, with some MPs promising abstentions in the House, and Robin Cook, Labour spokesman on health, was vocal about the Government's 'great thickness of skin'. The Prime Minister, Margaret Thatcher, was intransigent in her view that the NHS did not merit increased funding; the problem was doctors 'clinging to restrictive practices and deeply entrenched attitudes' which prevented moves for greater efficiency in the hospital sector. She claimed a great increase under her Government's regime in the numbers of operations carried out and in the through-put of patients in hospitals, whilst berating the doctors responsible for them for their laziness. *The Guardian* agreed that there were vested interests that needed to be challenged: 'That familiar fictional character, the over mighty consultant, bullying and exploiting subordinates and impervious to the rights of patients ... exists [but there was] ... daily evidence from the battlefield that the hospital service is coming close to breakdown.'[2]

In fierce debates in the House of Commons, Neil Kinnock, Leader of the Opposition, quoted Hoffenberg extensively in his attacks on the Government, and these continued into the January sittings. In the Press Hoffenberg reiterated that 'the whole reason for our statement was to ask for a proper review of the system'. The next phase was a meeting between John Moore, Secretary of State for Social Services, and Hoffenberg, Pinker and Todd. Moore listened patiently to their proposals and stated that he would do his best both to institute a proper review and to gain a substantial increase in funding. However, in the event Moore publicly denied 'he had conceded the need for additional resources for the health service'; he had clearly been overruled by Mrs Thatcher, his ministerial career plummeted, and John Major at the Treasury declared 'there ought to be no expectations of further additions to public expenditure'.[3]

In these debates various other options were canvassed: increased private health insurance together with tax relief on the payment of premiums, the contracting of routine operations from public to private hospitals, various efficiency savings, and greater involvement of doctors in administration. Hoffenberg suggested that as alcohol and tobacco-related illnesses 'placed such incredible burdens on the NHS, it would seem absolutely right that people who use the health service through personal abuse should be required to contribute towards costs through additional taxation on alcohol and tobacco'. The Presidents of the three Royal Colleges were of course disappointed by Moore's apparent *volte face* over funding and by the failure of the Government to announce a proper independent review. Hoffenberg said: 'We deprecate the approach of applying Elastoplast to stop a sore to the point where the whole body becomes covered in plasters, but new sores keep erupting.'[4]

These issues were kept alive in Britain during 1988, and on 3 October the Royal College of Physicians entertained Mrs Thatcher to lunch. The occasion was marked by continuous bickering. The Prime Minister felt she could not go to constituents asking them to find additional charges, whilst Hoffenberg ('with respect, Prime Minister') asked why French and German citizens were prepared to tolerate a much greater public expenditure on health care or why, within the OECD (Organisation for Economic Co-operation and Development), the UK health spending relative to GNP was the lowest of any country except Spain and Greece. Mrs Thatcher continued her accusations of the selfishness and laziness of the medical profession, its exploitation of young doctors and its duplication of services. When Hoffenberg helped her back into her car, her parting words were: 'You won't expect a letter of thanks from me for the lunch, will you?'[5]

The Conservative Government issued a White Paper, 'Working for Patients', in February 1989. Hoffenberg regarded it as a badly thought out, rushed job, based on an internal departmental committee which declared a position only after Mrs Thatcher's direct intervention set the parameters. The Council of the Royal College of Physicians stated that 'the Government was trying to apply free market policies to a state-run system

With Margaret Thatcher and College Officers in the President's Office before lunch. David Pyke, College Registrar (*far left*) and Tony Dawson, Treasurer (*far right*). 1988.

which employed 900,000 and the changes could neither be implemented as quickly nor in the manner proposed in the White Paper'. Hoffenberg believed that while, for example, in London there might be 13 kidney dialysis centres susceptible to some competition, the concept of competition could not apply, for instance, to Oxford, where there was one kidney unit. He saw the Paper as aimed simply at controlling costs; it was neither directed to improved patient care nor to better medical training, and he suggested 'the College would take the line that it welcomed and supported the objectives, but had doubts about the proposed methods of achieving them, and would now want to enter into constructive negotiations with the Government, with any reforms introduced initially as a pilot scheme'.

The College stated that the White Paper provided new and improved opportunities for the organization of local services, since greater regional autonomy was proposed, but that these changes may not necessarily be in the interests of the patients. It then worked with the other eleven Royal Medical Colleges to prepare a joint document dealing with patient care, the training of doctors and the need for security of resources for medical research. Eventually the unworkable aspects of some of the White Paper's proposals led to their withdrawal, and other savings and alternative managerial systems were introduced. An additional £2 billion was allocated to the NHS in the year following the review. Although Hoffenberg had been trenchant in his attacks on the Government, it is clear from his other writings that he understood that expenditure on health care had to be considered in the context of the competing demand for resources devoted to education, housing, transport and defence. Nevertheless, in 1994 he again attacked the level of NHS funding and the limits of the ethos of competition in providing health care.[6]

Health administration

Of the many issues of health administration which engaged Hoffenberg, the introduction of generic drugs in the NHS was one which considerably enhanced efficiency. From 1 April 1985 the Government intended to limit the range of drugs available for prescription in order to ensure that the cheapest version of the required drug was used, and to reduce the level of prescribing in situations where medical intervention was considered inappropriate. The British Medical Association proposed to boycott the measure on the grounds that it infringed a doctor's freedom to prescribe. The pharmaceutical lobby, which had representatives on the College's Appeal Committee that raised funds for the College's work, was vocally negative, since it perceived that its financial interests were threatened. However, Hoffenberg believed the British Medical Association's stance was foolish, and presented the College view: 'With certain reservations we approve the principle underlying the Government's proposals ... we support the idea of using cheaper drugs, providing their quality is assured.' The College 'considered the National Formulary Committee would be the correct body to draw up the list of the relevant drugs,' which should be under regular review, that appeal processes should be in place to safeguard physicians' interests, and that the list should cover all therapeutic needs. These proposals were accepted by the Government, which still had to bear the criticism of the Edinburgh Royal College of Physicians; the latter then received some generous sponsorships from drug companies for its work.[7]

Hoffenberg was drawn into a controversy about the use of drugs in 'alternative' or 'complementary' medicine. To him, the important question was whether they work. He maintained that we should not expect to *know how* they work before we sanction their use; physicians used penicillin and vaccination before the mechanisms of treatment were fully understood. He also observed that the outcome of other forms of alternative medicine – such as manipulation, stimulation (including acupuncture), relaxation and counselling, and even procedures such as 'aroma therapy' – were influenced by the emotional state of the patient, as was especially evident in the treatment of asthma. He noted that practitioners of alternative medicine usually spent more time with their patients than did traditional physicians.[8]

As President of the London College, Hoffenberg was obliged to attend many quasi-governmental committee meetings – as well as the working parties and committees of the College (described in chapter 8). The Standing Medical Advisory Committee of the DHSS (now Department of Health) had a wide brief. Its role was to offer strategic advice on issues identified by members as particularly significant to the medical profession. One of the issues in Hoffenberg's time was the need for inspection of institutions for the care of the elderly. He found the Joint Consultants Committee of the British Medical Association especially testing: the somewhat aggressive trade union approach of the BMA would lead to attacks in the morning on the Colleges, whose emphasis was on standards of patient care, and in the afternoon on the DHSS, in an attempt to secure better pay and conditions. The Awards Committee gave graded awards which influenced individual consultant salaries in the NHS; Hoffenberg was often at odds with committee members who valued length of service rather than scientific, academic or professional distinction, or who favoured a particular smaller specialty such as anaesthesia. Hoffenberg – the former lance-corporal – chaired the Armed Services Committee (comprising mainly Generals, Admirals and Air Vice-Marshals) which made consultant appointments in the defence forces. He considered the work of the Manpower Planning Committee to be especially futile, because of the opposition of both the British Medical Association and the Thatcher Government to increasing the numbers of doctors entering the profession. It was difficult to plan in detail the number of consultants in each specialty required in each region when posts were being left unfilled. These attitudes led to the massive shortage of doctors in Britain in the 1990s and the subsequent great expansion of training.[9]

In his book *Clinical Freedom*, Hoffenberg explored in some depth the conflict that physicians experienced in meeting a duty to the State for the equitable and efficient use of health resources and the duty of care for every individual patient in their charge.

> In the UK the combination of rising costs of services and rising demands for care has led to a system of rationing and queuing ... While queuing is a function of the recipient of health services, rationing is a function of the donor, in most cases the doctor. Does acceptance of this function compromise our clinical freedom? It is not easy to identify or isolate the part played by awareness of costs when individual doctors, GPs or consultants, decide whether or not to investigate or treat a patient. The open and direct opinion, 'This would cost too much' is rarely expressed and, I suspect, not often consciously entertained as a discretionary factor ... A more important question from the point of view of clinical freedom is whether and to what extent doctors are prevented from doing something they wish to do for their patients by an authoritarian embargo based on resource considerations which is in conflict with their professional judgement.

Hoffenberg referred to the differences in medical philosophy on the two sides of the Atlantic. There was a tendency in the USA to continue treatment until there is no further chance of success or benefit to the patient, whilst in the UK the emphasis was on whether treatment should be withdrawn or not offered to patients for whom it would have little or no benefit, or where the side effects may prove harmful. One attempt to produce a formula to quantify the relative benefits of treatment was to relate 'quality-adjusted life years' (QALYS) – the expected additional outcome for a patient's life from the exercise of a particular procedure – to the cost of treatment. Hoffenberg was sceptical of this somewhat simplistic approach to assisting doctors or health managers to make humane decisions; in wider debates ethicists believed it should be applied only sparingly in clinical decision-making and may work to the detriment of the least well-off. He wrote:

> It is in the field of acute hospital medicine that the conflict becomes most starkly real. For here decisions are no longer being taken in the abstract – they

apply to real patients whose fate – life or death – is in the balance. It is one thing for the responsible doctor to understand that 'obtaining scarce resources for an individual patient clearly reduces their availability to others'; it is quite another to expect him to explain to his patient that treatment which might be life-saving cannot be made available because of costs.

Hoffenberg was concerned that the management of health services was in the hands of staff who lacked any medical training and that decisions affecting patient care were being taken by politicians, administrators and economists. However, doctors were reluctant to enter management; in 1986 one of 14 NHS Regional Managers was medical; and 15 of 191 District Managers and 103 of 612 Unit Managers were medical. The College introduced courses in management for doctors and in medicine for managers. His view was that:

> Doctors are best placed to shift the emphasis of managerial enquiry from its pre-occupation with resources and costs to health outcome and patient satisfaction. For this reason alone medical participation in management is imperative. By ensuring that resources are devoted optimally to serve the interests of patients, doctors will find that their own clinical freedom is maximised.[10]

The Prison Medical Service

The Department of Health and Social Services asked the Royal College of Physicians to review the Prison Medical Service. Hoffenberg took this up as a serious challenge and assembled a working party which included Robin Murray, a distinguished psychiatrist whose specialty was criminology. The group visited seven prisons and took evidence from a wide range of people within and without the Prison Medical Service. They noted the isolation of the prison doctors but also the impracticality of combining the Service with the NHS. Many of the prison hospital wings were in bad shape and the English prison environment was generally depressing, marked by dilapidated buildings, inadequate sanitary arrangements and some overcrowding. Chronic ill health was prevalent, expressed mainly in personality disorders, psychiatric illness, epilepsy, sexually transmitted disease such as HIV and hepatitis B virus; there were also alcoholic and drug-related problems.

The particular features of medical practice were:

> The unselected and complex presentations of illness and dysfunction involving physical, psychiatric and social factors; many prisoners came from a deprived population ... For many inmates, imprisonment contributed to and focused attention on their symptoms, and many prisoners lacked the habits and skills of self-care.

The prisoners' health was clearly affected by the physical and operational features of the prison environment. The doctors were employees of the Prison Service and the doctor–patient relationship was therefore unusual.

In their final report the working party noted the limited opportunity for the training of doctors for what should be regarded as a specialty. They proposed a completely altered structure in which young doctors, recruited on the basis of their special aptitude, would enter training programmes; there would need to be a Joint Accreditation Board in Prison Medicine which could grant certificates. Career progression should be available, together with study leave. However, these recommendations were completely undermined by an appendix to the report from John L. Kilgour, Director of Prison Medical Services, who regarded training and an Accreditation Board as incompatible with the recruitment of experienced medical officers. Kilgour relied heavily on part-time GPs, often elderly, who lived near the prisons in question but lacked appropriate training or experience. His negative approach was supported by his successor, Dr Rosemary Wool, and the working party's recommendations for the reform of a serious societal problem were quietly buried. Dame Margaret Turner-Warwick, who was to be the next President of the Royal College, observed that whereas this Government asked for independent advice it was not genuine about wanting to taking that advice.[11]

Issues of public health

Preventive medicine should be seen as an attractive, cost-effective alternative to the expensive treatment of much ill-health endemic in the community. Nevertheless, in the face of long hospital waiting lists and escalating costs of treatment, governments are reluctant to consign resources to educational and other programmes that would help to alleviate many of the problems caused by poor health. Just occasionally, financial trade-offs can be made. In 1984 Hoffenberg visited Barney Heyhoe, Minister of State (Civil Service) and the Treasury, and on behalf of the College asked for a substantial increase in taxation on tobacco as a means of further discouraging smoking. He also saw Norman Fowler, Minister for Health. That year higher taxation on tobacco was a feature of the March Budget.[12] This was especially gratifying to the College as it had been one of the first institutions in a report in 1962 to publicise the link between smoking and ill-health; lung cancer and heart disease were the key syndromes. The College has also been and remains at the forefront in warning of the dangers of over consumption of alcohol. Hoffenberg chaired a group which in 1987 produced a report: *A Great and Growing Evil: The Medical Consequences of Alcohol Abuse*. Of all those 'consequences', the media chose to pick up Hoffenberg's statement at the press conference that heavy drinking led to reduced libido – expressed in banner headlines in the *Sun* newspaper as 'Drink'll wrinkle your winkle!.[13]

In 1983 the College produced a report on the dangers of obesity. These dangers were beyond question, but Hoffenberg was ambivalent about much of the nutritional advice on offer and aware of the continual shifts in scientific fashion. Whereas the nutrition of sheep and cattle has become an exact science, human nutrition has been unable to benefit from the same sophistication of research method, especially in a social climate which increasingly imposes ethical constraints on the procedures acceptable in human research. In early 1945 Hoffenberg had contracted hepatitis whilst campaigning in Italy and was flown to a hospital in Naples. He recalled:

> In those days it was thought necessary to rest in bed and have a very strict fat-free diet. Nothing is worse than food with no fat at all, but the man in the bed next to me was an Englishman who had kidney disease and he was on a protein-free diet. We quickly came to an arrangement and shared our meals. Neither of us came to any harm and this was the start of my scepticism about strict diet as part of medical treatment.[14]

In June 1984 Hoffenberg declared his reservations in the media, urging a distinction between 'advice that is based on sound evidence and that which is less secure and therefore a matter of opinion'. He wrote in 1988:

> Advice about diet is still not wholly agreed within the profession. A low fat or low salt diet is not likely to do harm and may do some good; the omission of sugar is not really thought to matter; the health-promoting qualities of fibre are increasingly being questioned; the use of whole-wheat bread, a preference for white wine or meat over red, or for bottled water over tap or for 'natural yoghurt' benefits only their producers and purveyors. The medical value of exercise, as opposed to the sense of well-being it might induce, is dubious. The nature of 'stress' is not understood or defined, and the benefits of avoiding it – even if this were possible – are obscure. To those who wish to live more 'healthily' could I offer four items about which I am convinced: 1. Don't smoke, 2. Don't drink too much, 3. Don't get too fat, 4. Don't waste your money on spurious and overpriced 'health foods'.[15]

He conceded variation in the response of individuals to particular dietary constituents, but cheerfully upset a number of lobbies in the above statement.

Hoffenberg was well aware of connections between socio-economic deprivation and morbidity and mortality, and was closely in touch with his presidential predecessor, Sir Douglas Black, on this issue. Black had chaired a group set up by the DHSS to study differences in health status among 'social classes'. It reported in 1980 – in *Inequalities in Health* – but its recommendations were largely rejected by the then new Conservative Government who sort to suppress its findings by printing only 260 copies of the report in a cheap format and publishing it on a Friday afternoon preceding a Bank holiday weekend when it would have the least exposure in the press.(Subsequently it was published by Penguin and received wide distribution). Black and his co-workers believed wealth and position assured 'better health education, medical attention and physical well-being, while less affluent classes enjoy less of the overall improvements in healthcare. Finally, cultural and behavioural factors need to be considered – diet, smoking, physical activities such as sport. The Report used 'occupational' rather than 'social' classes: professional (I), intermediate – managers, nurses, school teachers (II), skilled (III), partly skilled (IV) and unskilled – cleaners, dock workers, labourers (V).

Hoffenberg sought to maintain interest in the issues raised in Black's report. In a review he wrote in 1983, he noted there was a gradation associated with occupational group for almost every disease and cause of death; mortality of babies at birth from families of unskilled workers was double that of babies of professional families. Adult deaths from accidents and respiratory disease showed the steepest gradient according to occupational group but a similar gradient was also evident for digestive, genitourinary and cardiovascular system failure. Chronic bronchitis occurred in six per cent of Class I patients and 26 per cent of Class V patients. Overall death rates for men in 1971 were 4.0 per 1,000 population for Class I and 9.9 for Class V. One of the most troubling conclusions of Hoffenberg's report was that despite an overall improvement in British health, the gap according to occupational group appeared to have widened over the years; there was greater inequality of mortality between groups of men of economically active age in 1970–1972 than in 1949–1953.

Hoffenberg also observed that those at the bottom end of the occupational classes made less use of the preventive services offered by the NHS – such as antenatal classes and immunization programmes. The advice of specialists in occupational medicine could reduce accidents at work and measures could be taken to reduce smoking and excessive alcohol consumption. A shift of resources towards community care, particularly towards the care of young children, the elderly or mentally handicapped had excellent justification, as had better acute medical services and primary care.[16] However, social inequality remains as a causative factor for ill-health and mortality.

In 1988 Hoffenberg noted that medical research had been largely ineffective in providing treatment for a number of major diseases: hardening of the arteries or their sudden obstruction, high blood pressure and strokes, cancer, degeneration of the joints, dementia and schizophrenia, whereas simple, effective preventive measures were available against many major illnesses; cessation of smoking and lung cancer being one example. In a trenchant reminder of society's dysfunctional organization he wrote:

The six World Health Organization killer scourges of the Third World – diphtheria, measles, poliomyelitis, tetanus, TB and whooping cough – could be eliminated if we diverted annually to their eradication what we spend on armaments every three hours.[17]

CHAPTER TEN

Medical ethics

The ethical conduct of medical practice was a major concern for Hoffenberg from the beginning of his career. How doctors approach and carry out their work is dictated largely by the traditions of their profession but also by the ethical principles laid down by the statutory and regulatory bodies that govern medical practice. These principles are constantly being reviewed and updated as medical science advances, the range of possible procedures increases, and the socio-legal and political framework develops in line with current thinking. The activities of organisations closely related to medicine, such as pharmaceutical companies, are also subject to ethical scrutiny. As President of the Royal College of Physicians, Hoffenberg set up working parties to address some of the ethical issues that were particularly salient to medicine at that time (see Chapter 8). He chaired the College's Ethics Committee that set up the first guidelines for local ethics committees responsible for approving the conduct of research on human subjects. As will be described later in this chapter, he was also involved in other forums concerned with medicine and ethics. He helped to establish the Medical Foundation for the Care of Victims of Torture in which he continued to play an active role throughout his life. He retained strong ties with South Africa, publicly questioning the use of African miners for a research project and, as his private papers show, gave tangible support to those who attempted to investigate the circumstances of the death of the activist Steve Biko. In 1994 Hoffenberg was appointed Professor of Medical Ethics at the University of Queensland.

The diagnosis of death

The diagnosis of death and the duty of care doctors owe to patients in the closing phases of life were issues that deeply concerned Hoffenberg. His stance on these questions, which was public and proactive, emanated from his final days as a physician at Groote Schuur Hospital, when he was asked to sanction the removal of a still-beating heart from a patient:

> This marked my own introduction to the dilemma at the end of 1967 when
> I was asked to pronounce whether the heart of a young man admitted under

my care with a subarachnoid haemorrhage [i.e. bleeding into the membrane enveloping the brain] could be removed; the second of Christian Barnard's patients, Dr Blaiberg, was waiting to receive it. I shall not describe the anguish of this decision, but I was aware of an expectant surgical team, a throng of journalists from all over the world gathered at the door of the Groote Schuur Hospital – and my feeling of total inadequacy to make a sensible scientific judgement. There were no accepted scientific criteria that allowed one to pronounce as dead a patient whose heart was still beating, although media and public response to the excitement of the world's first transplant a few weeks earlier suggested that the procedure of removing a beating heart was not itself entirely unacceptable. After a sleepless night and three visits to the bedside to satisfy myself that there were no signs of life (other than a beating heart) I acceded to the request.[1]

Hoffenberg was put under some pressure to hasten his decision from one member of the surgical team who cried: 'God! What sort of a heart are you going to give us, Bill?'[2]

Subsequently the medical profession gave much thought to developing a set of criteria for the diagnosis of death. Whatever the philosophical arguments, Hoffenberg knew that it was important to reach a practical consensus on the problem.[3] In 1976 the Conference of Medical Royal Colleges declared death to be coincident with the death of the brainstem which results in irreversible loss of consciousness and the loss of capacity for spontaneous respiration; after long discussions the Colleges agreed the detailed criteria for a diagnosis of brainstem death.[4] Nevertheless, some members of the medical profession had their reservations. For example, in a paper entitled 'Against brainstem death,' the author argued for 'the place which the beating heart has in our culture's conception of the life and death of a human being' and stated that 'values rooted in our cultural and moral traditions stand beyond theoretical explanation'; why should the lack of persistent breathing have precedence over a beating heart?[5] Hoffenberg dismissed this type of argument and vigorously defended the Colleges' position.

In 1988 Hoffenberg chaired another group under the auspices of the Medical Royal Colleges to consider the problems of diagnosing death in the newborn, and advocated that where organs of a baby might be used for transplant the doctors making the diagnosis must not be members of the transplant team.[6]

Hoffenberg's interest in organ transplantation led him to help set up the International Forum for Transplant Ethics. The Forum emphasised the need for better education for doctors and nurses to enable them to be completely confident that all the criteria had been met when making a diagnosis of death; it was also essential that the diagnosis should be made quickly if organs were to remain viable for transplant. A survey of health-care professionals in Cleveland Ohio confirmed Hoffenbergs perception that there was widespread ignorance of the legal and medical criteria for determining death. Thirty-eight percent of those surveyed mistakenly regarded a patient in a permanent vegetative state as dead.[7] Other papers also quoted by Hoffenberg pointed to the confusion that then surrounded the diagnosis of death which had led to a considerable number of patients being maintained on life support when clinical criteria would have supported a diagnosis of death.[8,9]

End of life issues in medical practice

The treatment of a person with a terminal illness poses many ethical dilemmas both for the medical profession and for society as a whole. In his Valedictory Lecture at Wolfson College, 'Live and let Die' Hoffenberg focussed on four issues concerning the end of life: 1. The withholding of medical treatment; 2. The withdrawing of (or foregoing) a medical procedure; 3. Assisting suicide; and 4. Active euthanasia.[10]

These issues are resolved according to the stance of those involved in making the decisions and the legal framework of society with respect to the sanctity of human life, the physician's duty of care to alleviate pain and suffering, the quality of the patient's life and the degree of discomfort that would be likely to be experienced through extended treatment. To these may be added uncertainty concerning the outcome of treatment, the autonomy of the patient in respect of their right to refuse medical procedures and the interests of the patient's family.[11]

Withholding or withdrawing medical treatment

Decisions on whether and how to treat patients who are nearing the end of their lives are made by doctors on a case-by-case basis – always in the best interest of the patient and usually following discussion with the patient's family. In 1987 Hoffenberg chaired a working party of the Royal College of Physicians convened to provide guidance on resuscitation following cardiopulmonary arrest. The working party held that: 'Resuscitation is not indicated for all patients who suffer a cardiac arrest. It is inappropriate to attempt to resuscitate those patients whose lives are drawing naturally to a close because of irreversible diseases.' (The working party also made recommendations that all doctors should be trained in resuscitation techniques – skills that had hitherto often been missing from their training.)[12]

Hoffenberg also considered the basis on which decisions should be made to withdraw medical treatment, for example from a patient who was being kept alive artificially with no hope of regaining consciousness. He advocated that in these circumstances giving medication which had a dual effect of reducing suffering and shortening life would be preferable to the gradual withdrawal of food and water. He queried whether court proceedings – often involving family members with different agendas – provided the best forum for decisions to be made on the withdrawal of life support. Following the Bland case (in which a patient in a permanent vegetative state had been maintained on life support for over four years) the House of Lords had recommended that decisions to withdraw life support should be under the court jurisdiction (Airedale NHS Trust v Bland [1993] 1All ER 821 HL). 'I don't mind denigrating legality at all' he commented in a throwaway line in his Wolfson lecture.

Patients have a right to refuse treatment; in fact the imposition of medical treatment against the wishes of the patient constitutes an assault in law. Hoffenberg emphasized the need for consent (in this case a decisions to refuse treatment) to be informed; he wrote:

> My belief is that these decisions must rest on a proper knowledge of all the medical consequences of each option, physical and psychological, qualitative as well as quantitative; that they must be made with critical and professional detachment, and that they should be conveyed to and discussed with the patient and the family with compassion and sensitivity.[13]

Where the patient has no understanding of their present circumstances an advance directive or 'living will' would provide guidance to the doctor.

Euthanasia

'Doctors have a moral and an ethical obligation to provide a peaceful, dignified death with minimal suffering. They have no obligation to do more and they cannot in fact legally do more.'[14] The death of Mrs Lilian Boys, who had been a patient of Dr Nigel Cox for twelve years, became a *cause célèbre*. She was in excruciating pain and asked for death, her two sons concurring. Massive doses of morphia had proved ineffective, and Cox, acting out of compassion, injected potassium chloride, which could have no therapeutic benefit. Cox was charged with attempted murder, was convicted but was given a suspended sentence. Hoffenberg gave evidence on behalf of Cox at the later General Medical Council hearing; Cox was reprimanded but his right to practise medicine was reinstated.[15]

The term euthanasia (literal meaning, an easy death) usually refers to the deliberate, active and intended termination of life by one individual at the request of another who does not wish to continue living. Hoffenberg believed that much was to be gained by debating euthanasia openly. In the early 1990s it was not permitted to practice euthanasia in any Western country, although in the Netherlands the Dutch parliament, whilst not legalizing euthanasia, had agreed that doctors would not be prosecuted if they followed a code of stringent guidelines. The 14 November 1991 issue of *The Independent* reported on a seminar which bore the headline 'Leading doctor urges legalising euthanasia'; it continued:

> Euthanasia should be legalized to enable chronically sick old people to die with dignity, a past president of the Royal College of Physicians said yesterday ... Euthanasia ... could be the right alternative to sustaining poor quality life for frail elderly people, provided it served the interests of patients and close family.

Hoffenberg however was misquoted, and Marshall Marinker, Director of the MSD Foundation, leapt to his defence: '... at no time did Sir Raymond suggest the legalising of euthanasia. Certainly he reported the position in the Netherlands, but he did so in order to open for more public debate the difficult ethical questions posed by "the right to die"'. Hoffenberg wrote to Roger Cobden-Ramsay of the legal firm, Radcliffes, stating that *The Independent* report was particularly damaging to his 'reputation as a spokesman on bioethical matters ... I fear that the attribution to me of such a radical statement will undermine my credibility as an impartial and open-minded ethicist'. He was especially concerned for his position as an adviser to St Christopher's Hospice, since the legalization of euthanasia was not compatible with the general objectives of hospice care. Radcliffes secured a retraction and the recovery of their costs from *The Independent*.[16]

In his Wolfson lecture[10] Hoffenberg suggested the important judgements were whether the patient's illness was terminal and how real and severe was the patient's anguish. The Institute of Medical Ethics, of which he became president, favoured medical euthanasia if the patient continually sought death. Yet legal euthanasia brought many problems; court disputes, division of relatives and caused suffering.

Hoffenberg found it difficult to discuss these and similar bioethical issues with those with rigidly held religious views.[17] He dismissed the view that ordained processes were paramount in controlling life, since accepted modern medical treatments clearly interfered with these processes. Different religious traditions gave differing weight to the sanctity of life as an absolute value in which physicians might be seen to have a duty to prolong life whatever the cost to the patient. It is of interest that although in the Rabbinic tradition 'every moment of life is to be cherished to the last', all Jewish doctors surveyed in a New South Wales study were positive about active voluntary euthanasia.[18]

Transplanting organs

From the time of his involvement with Christian Barnard's first heart transplant at Groote Schuur hospital in 1967, Hoffenberg took a keen interest in the ethics of organ transplantation and both advocated and activated some radical protocols designed to reduce the shortages in organ supply, which he presented to both lay, and scientific and medical audiences. He chaired a working party of the Medical Royal Colleges which in 1987 reported on approaches to increasing the supply of donor organs. Although the criteria for brain stem death had been established, fears remained in some quarters that organs might be taken from patients who were not dead and the fears of the general public were heightened by slanted media coverage. Hoffenberg sought wider public education on these issues. He wrote in *The Times* that:

> ... the lives of many patients are being jeopardized by 'irrational and unfounded' allegations about the conduct of transplant teams ... which could lead to a severe cutback in the public response to the need for donor organs for adults and children who would otherwise die ... There is no possibility of organs being taken from a patient who is still alive.[19]

In the mid-1990s Hoffenberg helped to bring together a distinguished multidisciplinary group to form the International Forum for Transplant Ethics (IFTE). The group comprised representatives of philosophy, anthropology and law as well as transplant surgeons and physicians, drawn from Boston and Montreal, from London, Liverpool and Oxford, as well as Oman. The *modus operandi* of the group was to investigate designated transplant issues and to meet for open-ended discussion until a consensus emerged which might be published. The starting point was 'the premise that any procedure that increased the supply of organs would be doing good by saving lives or improving the quality of life for the recipient, unless it is inherently and incorrigibly associated with consequences that outweigh its benefits'.[20]

Hoffenberg and the Forum believed that ethical questions of what is right, good or just in human conduct should be examined *de novo* and not initially conflated with social, religious or professional tradition. Neither should unwillingness to examine such issues be justified by an immediate response such as human revulsion; some of the legislation restricting organ donation had been introduced on the basis of intuitive responses rather than reasoned debate.

Consenting to the donation of organs

The procedures adopted before organs are removed from a dead person vary greatly between countries. In the UK the system is one of 'contracting in', where the patient is known to have consented to future donation of organs and there is no express objection by relatives. In Belgium consent is presumed unless the patient has expressly declared an objection to organ removal, but in practice the relatives are consulted – a 'soft' form of 'contracting out'; the primary role of relatives is to corroborate that the dead person did not actually register an objection. In Austria there is a 'hard' form of presumed consent and organ removal is carried out irrespective of the relatives' views.[21]

Hoffenberg was among those who believed that the UK, which had a low kidney donation rate (13 per million persons per year), should legislate to change to the 'presumed consent' model. There are grounds for believing this would increase the rate of kidney donation, as it had done in Spain, Austria and Belgium after legislation for presumed consent was introduced. Hoffenberg wrote:

> The Conference of European Health Ministers and the World Health Organization have supported the Belgian model in which the views of relatives are not ignored. Experience with 'contracting out' legislation has shown that by and large the public is comfortable with it. There seems no reason any longer not to adopt it.[22]

But Hoffenberg's views have not been accepted and the question remains one of considerable debate. [23]

The sale of organs

In most countries the sale of kidneys is banned and until recently the donation of a kidney from an unrelated person was banned.[23] Despite this, there is a significant international trade in organs and many Westerners travel abroad to obtain a kidney transplant. Hoffenberg believed the forms of restrictive legislation that prevented the sale of organs should be subject to ethical scrutiny. In an unpublished paper he put forward controversial but reasoned arguments as to why most of the objections to the sale or donation of kidneys from an unrelated donor, when considered purely logically and in the context of the needs and attitudes of potential donors should be revised.[24,25] To the argument 'that it is degrading to have to sell an organ in order to get badly needed money', Hoffenberg's response was that poverty is the primary degradation to be attacked, rather than the autonomy of the donor. 'These arguments seem more designed to protect Western sensibilities from distress in contemplating the fate of the would-be paid donor in the developing world, rather than to solve his or her problems.' Hoffenberg also countered arguments on exposure to risk, increased criminality, coercion and consent. He suggested that the establishment of an intermediate agency between purchaser and vendor might maintain health standards and promote equity of allocation.

Prisoners as organ donors for transplantation

Hoffenberg raised the possibility that some prisoners would be prepared to donate a kidney if this led to some remission of their sentence. He queried whether this avenue should be closed to them? The difficult issues of possible coercion and the validity of consent for this vulnerable group were emphasised by a Royal College of Physicians working party on research on healthy volunteers chaired by him in 1986.[26]

The removal of organs from executed prisoners was widely practised in China and has been discussed with great repugnance in Western countries. Hoffenberg, having once asked whether prisoners might not reasonable seek expiation of their crime through kidney donation, insisted that two ethical questions should not be conflated: the death penalty, which he opposed and which is now prohibited in most European countries, and the issue of whether after an execution the prisoner's organs might be removed to alleviate the suffering of another individual

Hoffenberg summarized the main arguments against organ donation from executed prisoners: (1) Prisoners may be executed to provide a source of organs. He believed that the range of offences attracting the death penalty in China was so wide and the supply of executed persons so great that this scenario was improbable. (2) The process of execution may be modified to facilitate the supply of effective transplants. (3) The autonomy of the prisoner in consenting to organ removal is unlikely to apply in the circumstances that surround executions. However this is an ethical question of much smaller moment than that of killing the person and should also be viewed in the context of the lesser weight given to the rights of the individual in Chinese culture. (4) Organs taken from executed prisoners may be sold for profit. It is the abuse of the system which should attract opprobrium rather than the legitimate and controlled removal of organs. (5) The role of doctors in the removal of organs is unacceptable to some professional bodies.[27]

Donations from unrelated persons

Although kidney transplantation from living, unrelated donors has a higher success rate than kidneys transplanted from cadavers, in many countries there are restrictions which prevent such arrangements. Hoffenberg pointed out that such restrictions could not be justified by their failure rate, especially when the growth of immunosuppressor technology had lessened the need for tissue matching. 'Kidney transplantation between living, unrelated donors is just as successful as between blood relatives matched for a single haplotype.'[28]

Hoffenberg believed that the argument that restricting donations to family members – as had been advocated by the government in 1989 – would avoid commercialism and coercion was unrealistic; one cannot assume that altruistic, unselfish love of the kind which leads to organ donation exists only within the family, or that the consent of family members is always freely given and never involves an unequal exchange of presents – something in return. 'Blood relations may be just as corruptible or open to pressure as non-relations.'

In most countries donations are permitted between spouses. It may be argued that close and dear friends and others should have the same opportunity to display their altruism freely. Hoffenberg wrote:

> A person who dives into the sea to rescue a drowning person or runs into a burning house to save a threatened child does not first check whether it is a blood relative. In both cases the risk to the rescuer is greater, but saving a life in this way is not banned by law or limited to those with genetic links. The fact that one action takes place in the heat of the moment, the other planned in cold blood, does not detract from the heroism, or altruism of both.

The organization and allocation of donated organs

The issue of allocating organs across ethnic boundaries was raised by Hoffenberg in 2003 in response to an article praising this bridging. He indicated that in 1967 the second heart transplant at Groote Schuur Hospital, given to the white dentist, Dr Phillip Blaiberg, came from a young black man of mixed race. He wrote:

> This transracial exchange was quite remarkable in a country that at the time kept separate blood banks for white and non-white blood and in which an occasional white patient was allowed to die rather than be transfused with 'black' blood or, for that matter, transported to hospital in a 'black' ambulance. How sad it is that transplants across ethnic or religious barriers are still regarded as remarkable ...[29]

The International Forum for Transplant Ethics was concerned that many studies of minority attitudes towards organ donation repeat conceptual and methodological errors that undermine their scientific value; race, ethnicity or culture may be conflated with biological variation. 'The commonly held view that minorities donate dramatically less than their representation in the population is in fact mistaken,' at least with respect to Afro-Americans in the USA, but their greater representation on the waiting list for kidneys suggests inequity and discrimination.[30]

Hoffenberg also emphasised the importance of organisational factors to successful transplant programmes: priorities were well trained staff, particularly specialist coordinators to liaise with families, better facilities and the need for more hospitals to join the donor network. All countries should set up central processing units that adhered to a rigorous set of standards for the collection, storage and transport organs.[31,32]

Research on South African miners

Research in South Africa on the tolerance of miners to heat stress attracted Hoffenberg's dismay in November 1969 when he wrote to the editor of the *Journal of Applied Physiology*, noting its endorsement of the Declaration of Helsinki:

> ...Yet, your issue of August 1969 contains an article by Strydom and Williams (p.262) which appears to conflict with these principles. The authors have submitted 'Bantu' subjects to intense physical exercise capable of increasing their pulse rates to over 160 beats per minute and their rectal temperatures to over 40°C. Their physical discomfort was perhaps aggravated by the indignity of having to perform these tasks 'in the nude'. Nowhere in this article is any mention made of 'informed consent' having been obtained. I think you should know that these young men are brought to work on the mines in South Africa under contract from remote rural areas ... I would doubt whether informed consent could have been obtained and, more important, whether awareness of the possible consequences of refusal to participate would not have made these men 'conscripts' rather than 'volunteers'. The attitude of these authors may perhaps be gauged by their reference on p.265 to 'these Bantu'. Would 'these men' or 'these subjects' not be more appropriate? One does not normally find references to 'these Jews' or 'these Negroes' in medical articles. It would be reassuring to know that your journal insisted on this type of human experimentation being conducted along the lines laid down by Helsinki.[33]

Donald S. Frederickson wrote to Professor N.B. Strydom expressing the Publication Committee's concern, and Strydom noted his 'regret and surprise' at 'the aggressive attitude and unfounded accusations of Dr Hoffenberg', claiming a humanitarian approach 'in improving the working and living conditions of the industry's Bantu labour force ... the only reason for not having [mention of informed consent in the article] is that the procurement of such consent is taken for granted in all our experiments'. Frederickson replied diplomatically that his committee accepted Strydom's assurances about the consent of the participants, but explained the safeguarding mechanisms operating in the USA; 'we are unaware of the existence of such institutional committees in South Africa'.[34]

C.H. Wyndham, Director of the Chamber of Mines of South Africa Research Organization, then wrote to Hoffenberg's superior, Sir Peter Medawar, complaining that Hoffenberg had written on National Institute for Medical Research paper and resenting his 'informed' criticism; Wyndham was apparently unaware of the good relations Hoffenberg enjoyed with Medawar and the degree of openness in the international scientific community outside South Africa. Hoffenberg had continued his close, personal relationship with his mentor Professor J.F. Brock at the University of Cape Town, and it was a bitter blow to him when Brock wrote expressing disappointment with Hoffenberg's 'so uninformed and so unfair' letter to the Journal which was 'unworthy of the high regard in which I have always held you'.[35] Brock's disappointment must have related to Hoffenberg's scepticism as to how informed consent might have been obtained, given the special relationship between investigator and 'volunteer'.

Hoffenberg's response merits extensive quotation, since it reveals much of his thinking at this time In referring to the modern concepts of the ethics of human experimentation expressed in the Declaration of Helsinki and the British Medical Research Council's statements, Hoffenberg wrote:

> In this particular case the matter goes much deeper. This research is not being done to provide information about a disease, to find a cure or to prevent a natural illness. It is [apparently] aimed at alleviation of suffering and danger imposed on man by his fellow men and, at the risk of being called cynical, I shall go further and question the reason for this imposition. The gold-mines in South Africa are its most lucrative source of revenue; this revenue is being used to create and maintain a system which, by ministerial pronouncement, is dedicated to white supremacy and total control of a black labour force. The research programme in question states as one of its objectives the desire to 'increase productivity of working' ... When investigators start to concern themselves with the degree of heat and the 'work-rate' that workers can tolerate, I begin to think of farmers calculating minimum feeding requirements for their cattle, or even of Nazis estimating how much their labour-forces could stand before they became unproductive ... What I should warn you about is that my attitude is shared by most people outside the country ... I know the arguments about benefits accruing to the blacks but ... any economic analysis will show quite clearly how the spoils are divided ...

Hoffenberg went on to refer to the changed focus on the rights and interests of patients and continued:

Of greater concern to me is your [Brock's] suggestion of disloyalty ... as a 'hater' of South Africa. Unlike all members of the Government and many others beside, I proved my loyalty to SA from 1942–1945 in North Africa and Italy. To the majority of South Africans I proved my loyalty by standing up for their rights and dignity. This I shall go on doing. The fact that I and my family have been deprived of our home, our birthright and my proper career will not stop me from stating privately or publicly what I feel – and this I do as an individual who has suffered deeply at the hands of a minority power-group, not as a member of any politically motivated organization ... and, once again for the record and your peace of mind, I have never indulged and will never indulge in any unlawful pursuit to bring about a change of government, even though I would dearly love to see it. I shall continue to protest whenever possible at those things I believe to be wrong. If we differ in our judgement of these, I am extremely sorry.

Brock responded with partial apologies, and with concurrence about ' the inhumanity of the present government'; eventually their relationship was repaired.[36]

Medicine and torture

Hoffenberg did not avoid the vexed issue of the widespread use of torture. He referred to his own dilemma in the 1950s when he discovered that a patient, a political activist, bore the residual marks of torture suffered in South African police custody.

Where a doctor knows or suspects that torture has taken or is taking place, what is one's professional duty? My patient begged me not to say anything, terrified that it might lead to further arrest and torture. I kept quiet and have felt uneasy about it ever since.

He sought to encourage the medical profession to become involved in alleviating this form of human suffering: He recognized that:

....even in recent years there have been innumerable accounts of torture from much of Africa, the Middle and Far East, the USSR and its constituent states, South America and Europe. In the UK in the early 1970s ... accounts of physical brutality against prisoners suspected of belonging to the IRA ... confirmed the use of prolonged forced standing, hooding, exposure to continuous noise, isolation and deprivation of sleep, food and water.[37]

These methods have since been prohibited in the UK.[38]

Hoffenberg became involved in the 1970s with the establishment of the Medical Foundation for the Care of Victims of Torture which operates a clinic in North London. In addition to physical repair, the approach is to move the survivor from a position of total dependence to one in which she/he is prepared to assume control over his/her own life and rehabilitation programme.[39]

Steve Biko

This account of the appalling Steve Biko case is drawn from Hoffenberg's articles in the *Journal of Medical Ethics* and the *European Review*. Biko, who founded the Black Consciousness Movement in South Africa, was 'physically imposing, intelligent, articulate and courageous', exhibiting natural leadership qualities. He was murdered in a police station in Hoffenberg's home town of Port Elizabeth in 1977; after arrest he was interrogated, tortured and sustained blows to the head which damaged his brain. A doctor examined him when he was dying and 'certified that he found no evidence of any abnormality or pathology'. Several days later the senior district surgeon observed Biko 'collapsed on the floor in an apathetic condition, incontinent, frothing at the mouth and hyperventilating, with a head injury and unequivocal clinical evidence of brain damage'. The doctor reported no positive evidence of organic disease but did recommend admission to hospital. When the commander of the security police refused to have Biko admitted locally, Biko was transported, handcuffed, in the back of a police Landrover 1,200 km to Pretoria, where he died the next day.

At the inquest the counsel for the Biko family described the relationship of the district surgeons to the police commander as 'one of subservience bordering on collusion'. The two doctors, Ivor Lang and Benjamin Tucker, 'totally abrogated their responsibility for the welfare of a prison inmate who had become their patient, ... and acted criminally by filling in false medical reports in order to hide the fact that he had been the victim of serious physical abuse'.

There followed a long and tortuous legal process of reviewing the conduct of the doctors. A woman friend of Hoffenberg's had mortgaged her home in order to meet the forecast legal expenses and Hoffenberg in Britain raised a fund of £30,000 from sympathizers. However eventually she won her case, she was awarded costs, and Hoffenberg had to write and explain the situation to the donors. They did not want their money back, which was used to establish the Steve Biko Fund, for which Hoffenberg was to give the first lecture.[40] Lang and Tucker were found guilty of disgraceful or improper behaviour and were struck off the medical register, eight years after the incidents. The South African Mental and Dental Council and the Medical Association of South Africa were slow to criticize the conduct of their members or conditions in prison, and Hoffenberg believed that the strong support of professional associations was necessary to help individual doctors maintain good ethical standards in the treatment of prisoners.

CHAPTER ELEVEN

Medical activist

Crossing the barrier

Although passionate and determined in pursuing the causes to which he was committed, Hoffenberg personally eschewed public demonstration as a means of achieving his aims. Rather he aimed to inform and educate. In his later professional life, having achieved high office, he usually worked to mobilize the resources available through channels of the Establishment. He was however, ready to adopt unpopular causes in the defence of human rights. He believed societal change should follow an individual's commitment to ethical stances, and observed:

> There is something curious that happens to some people. They have to cross a certain barrier, a line in their lives. Until then they tend to live contented quiet lives without concerning themselves about broader issues. But at some stage they do cross the line, and then all sorts of things fall into place and they begin to concern themselves more in the health or welfare of communities. The task is to get people to cross the line.[1]

Hoffenberg accepted leading roles in a plethora of wide-ranging organisations and enjoyed their diversity. They spanned cancer, heart disease, mental illness, provincial hospitals, medical research, antinuclear warfare, victims of torture and refugee academics. Some observers commented that he could hardly have made an effective contribution in so many fields; however, with the back-up of many distinguished individuals in the roles of vice-president or vice-chair, it is generally agreed that his contributions to the organisations he represented were effective and much valued. His workaholic, driven character, his very long working hours – having risen at dawn he continued to work at home on most evenings – and his very efficient use of time all helped him to sustain his prolific output, whilst his intellect, wit and charm made him an influential and effective operator. His physical fitness and athleticism also contributed to the sheer energy needed to play an active part in so many organisations and causes.

Cancer and heart disease

Hoffenberg was serving on the council of the large, well endowed Imperial Cancer Research Fund when the Department of Health and Social Services and the Medical Research Council asked him to accept the larger task of chairing the UK Cancer Committee for Coordinating Research. This committee provided an umbrella for the different bodies working with cancer, monitoring their operations to ensure that their work was being directed appropriately and that they were efficient and focused.

The Committee's activities included the support of joint research projects – for example the initiation and funding of working groups on cancer risk in workers in biology laboratories – and various clinical trials. These were overseen by a series of committees: trials, site-specific (breast, colorectal, gynaecological, lung) and a radiation and cancer group. Their work embraced preventive medicine, for example breast screening, and the production of educational reports. The Committee also acted as a lobby group, for example continually harassing ministers about the dangers of smoking – and oral snuff – and engaging the media in these issues. There were many links with other cancer bodies, for example, the committees on Cancer Registration and on Animals in Research, and several European and international bodies. This broad canvas tested Hoffenberg's organizational skills and the disparate bodies, whilst retaining their separate identities, usually worked together harmoniously in seeking to confront the scourge of cancer.[2]

There was a further contretemps with Margaret Thatcher in 1990. Her husband Denis had been a patient at St Thomas' Hospital in London and Mrs Thatcher, pleased with his treatment there, asked his surgeon if there was anything he needed. He asked for a cyclotron to deliver a low-energy form of neutron therapy, specifically for head and neck cancer. Mrs Thatcher, without further consultation, ordered that this be purchased; the cost was £6 million. Hoffenberg, as chair of the UK Cancer Coordinating Committee for Research, talked with his colleagues. They were sceptical of the efficacy of this type of therapy and aware of its adverse side effects; moreover, experimentation was still ongoing. In May 1990 Hoffenberg spoke to the press, stating that it was believed that more than 30 patients in the USA had died from this treatment. The NHS, which had been nervous about the project from its inception, sent three specialists to the USA where this form of neutron therapy had by then been abandoned; their report was negative and the proposal was quietly buried.[3]

In September 1987 Hoffenberg succeeded Sir Cyril Clarke, former President of the Royal College of Physicians, as chair of the Council of the British Heart Foundation, the third largest UK research charity after the two major cancer organizations. For six years he raised funds for research and education and guided the work of the Foundation, which was responsible for the establishment of about 20 Heart Foundation University Chairs as well as many trainee fellowships and long- and short-term research grants. In 1993 a coordinating committee for cardiac disease was established along similar lines to the cancer coordinating committee. However, this did not work well, owing to competing interests from within cardiology. Hoffenberg chaired only two meetings before leaving for Australia.[4]

Mental health

In Britain, during the 1980s, many institutions for the care of the mentally ill – whose practices could often have been described as Draconian – had been closed, but their replacement by more appropriately run centres and 'half-way houses', though offering gentler more empathic regimens, proved inadequate, as did the support provided in the community for the mentally disadvantaged. Hoffenberg became President of the Mental Health Foundation in 1989, at the time the government's 'Caring for People' White Paper was published. The Foundation's main committee was directed to identify 'the needs of people with long-term mental illness in the community, the needs of families and carers, and the provision and evaluation of services'. Account was therefore taken of the views of the users of these services and the long-term needs of the professionals and carers seeking to adapt to the newly reorganized NHS.

A second specialist group was concerned with how best to meet the needs of people with a mental handicap and challenging behaviour such as 'self injury, aggression, destruction of the environment and stereotyped behaviour which may be dangerous'. Its agenda embraced issues of patient restraint, the creation of special environments, the use of drugs in therapy and behaviour therapy.

Hoffenberg took office when Major General R.B. Loudon, who over 15 years had raised the Foundation's income from £0.25 to £2.5m per annum, was retiring. Peter Searle assumed the Directorship. HRH Princess Alexandra was an active Patron and some leading industrialists were involved. With their help Hoffenberg hosted a successful fundraising Fortieth Anniversary at the Café Royal in London.

One innovation made during Hoffenberg's term of office was the establishment of a bail hostel in Birmingham for mentally disordered defendants. Its purpose was to keep mentally ill people out of prison while on remand. The venture was partly supported by the NHS. About 100 bail hostels – but with a wider brief – were eventually established. The

Robert Loder, Vice President of the UK Mental Health Foundation with Bill, its President, 1989.

Foundation also produced an influential report on the management of mentally disturbed offenders. A Music Therapy Centre was set up in North Yorkshire and the Foundation instigated some innovative educational programmes; for example, it supported the production of a play, 'Cracked', to assist awareness of mental health issues. Research projects funded included studies of dementia, and the training of GPs 'to make a more effective response to the psychiatric and emotional needs of patients'.[5]

Nuffield Trust

The Nuffield Provincial Hospitals Trust, as it was then known, worked to improve health care in the provinces outside London. Hoffenberg served as an influential Trustee for four years from July 1989, when Sir Maurice Shock was Chairman. Earlier, in 1986, the Trust had invited Hoffenberg to the deliver the Rock Carling Lecture; he chose to speak on clinical freedom.

The Trust had an annual income of about £1.8 million which it directed to a wide range of activities that included support for the provision and improvement of medical services, medically related research projects and educational activities. During Hoffenberg's tenure, the Trust's work, initiated and moved forward by its Secretary, Michael Ashley-Miller, focused on ways of meeting the health care needs of people with physical disabilities and issues of advocacy for young disabled adults. Some of the programmes funded by the Trust were directed to improving services for rehabilitation for people who were deaf and losing their sight, investigations into the quality of care delivered to the frail elderly, and people with spinal injuries living at home. A manual on the rehabilitation services available for young people was produced. Future directions in nursing and primary health care, and research on the aetiology of Alzheimer's disease also received the Trust's attention and chairs were established in Community Care Studies at Glasgow and Leicester Universities. Hoffenberg enthusiastically supported these initiatives and upon his retirement as a Trustee it was said that 'the Trust will miss the breadth and depth of experience he brought to bear in discussion, as well as his wide-ranging network of contacts and his own inimitable style and wit'.[6]

Wolfson Foundation

Hoffenberg greatly admired Sir Isaac Wolfson, one of thirteen children of a Russian immigrant, who described himself simply as 'a Jewish boy from the gorbals' of Glasgow. In his youth he had worked as a hawker on the London-Glasgow train and, in later life as a party trick, would recite all the stations on that route. His business acumen eventually led to the creation of Great Universal Stores and to other commercially successful ventures. In 1955 he established the Wolfson Foundation which supported the advancement of health, education and youth activities. He is believed to have said: 'No man needs more than £100 thousand a year to live comfortably; the rest should be given away.' Only Jesus and Mary Magdalene share the distinction of having Colleges bearing their name at both Oxford and Cambridge – there are Wolfson Colleges in both cities. Sir Isaac, when asked why he was awarded an honorary degree, responded that it was 'for writing'; actually for writing cheques. His death in June 1991 was marked by a memorial service at the Central Synagogue in Great Portland Street, London.[7]

With the endorsement of Lord (Leonard) Wolfson, Sir Isaac's son, Hoffenberg wrote Sir Isaac's entry in the *Munk's Roll* of the Royal College of Physician which records lives of all deceased Fellows of the College; Sir Isaac had been made an Honorary Fellow. He referred to the Wolfson Foundation's support for medicine, and to its major initiatives for the care of the blind, the disabled, for hospices and hospitals, for preventive medicine, and medical education and research. The Royal College of Physicians had been a prime beneficiary, and in 1959 received £450,000 towards the cost of its new building in Regent's Park as well as support for its research unit, led first by Sir Cyril Clarke, a past president of the

131

College, and then by Dr Anthony Hopkins. Hoffenberg went on to describe Sir Isaac as follows:

> Physically on the small side, he was larger than life as a person – warm, generous, kind, humorous – with a gift for making people relax and laugh. He was deeply religious but his charitable philosophy was based on a wider appreciation of the need to help those less fortunate than himself ... Sir Isaac will be remembered as one of the great philanthropists of modern times. We in medicine have particular cause to be grateful.[8]

Hoffenberg succeeded Sir Cyril Clarke as a trustee of the Foundation and served under the chairmanship of Lord Wolfson for over six years from February 1987. By 1994 the assets of the Foundation approximated £466 million, with an annual income of £14 million. During the later years of Hoffenberg's term the Foundation spent about half its grants on research and technology, and increased the medical component in these areas, whilst about one-fifth went to education. A further fifth went to the arts and humanities, mainly benefiting historians, libraries, the conservation of historic buildings, and museums and galleries.

Hoffenberg had special responsibilities for the Foundation's spending on health and welfare. When reporting to it in 1991 he referred to the increasing cost of sophisticated medical treatment which necessarily diverted public funds 'from what may broadly be termed "welfare" activities'. It was in such areas of healthcare that the Foundation had given special support, helping to establish an institute of preventive medicine, a school of public health, and an institute of child health. Grants had been made to almost 40 hospices in recognition that much can be done to relieve the physical and mental suffering of the terminally ill and to support their families; a lectureship had been established at Leeds to teach doctors about terminal care. Special grants were also made for the care of children. Hoffenberg's understanding of the operations of the Foundation was helpful in enabling other institutions with which he was involved, such as the Society for the Protection of Science and Learning, to submit successful grant applications to the Wolfson Foundation.[9]

Refugee academics

The World University Service, a relief organization concerned with students, academics and universities experiencing difficulties, had first engaged Hoffenberg's concern in South Africa where he was its president until 1967 (as mentioned in chapter 4). Later, in Birmingham, he renewed his interest and became its vice-president in Britain. He represented the Service on the council of management of the Society for the Protection of

Science and Learning, becoming its president in 1991 following the resignation of Lord Eric Ashby. Sir Anthony Kenny, Warden of Rhodes House, subsequently stepped down as chairman. Hoffenberg then combined the two roles until1993 when the prospect of going to Australia led him to prevail upon Professor Shula Marks to take the chair.[10]

The Society has a long and illustrious history. When Hitler came to power in 1933 William Beveridge, a leading economist and social reformer, stimulated the formation of an Academic Assistance Council, renamed in 1936 the Society for the Protection of Science and Learning. It helped to bring refugee academics to Britain and to find work for them. They came mainly from Germany and Austria; many had lost their posts because of their Jewish ancestry. The movement to assist them had wide support from the academic community, even though distinguished professors coming from abroad could be perceived as adding to the competition for the limited number of British academic and research positions. The activities of the Society significantly enriched Britain's cultural, academic and scientific life, despite the negative perceptions of many people in the UK government. An archive delivered to the Bodleian Library in 1988 lists the wide range of subject disciplines augmented by refugees: from archaeology and art history to biology, chemistry and mathematics; from philosophers including Martin Buber, Raymond Klibansky and Karl Popper to physicists such as Arthur Beer, Max Born, Rudolf Peierls and Edward Teller. The Society could count from among the refugees it had helped, or their children, 16 Nobel Laureates, 77 Fellows of the Royal Society and 34 Fellows of the British Academy.[11]

However, in 1940 the anxieties and insecurities of wartime led to the internment of great numbers of refugee academics. The Secretary of the Society, Esther (Tess) Simpson, was pivotal to its activities for nearly five decades. She was unremitting in her search for the interned academics and instrumental in the release of some five hundred of them. One of the more bizarre sidelights in a book about her life[12] is a facsimile reproduction of a letter vouching for 'the perfect loyalty to this country' of a refugee art historian, signed by the art historian, Anthony Blunt, who was later exposed as a spy for the Soviet Union. Tess Simpson was a remarkable person whose warm hearted compassion and gift for friendship were matched by tireless determination and administrative efficiency. She was a gifted violinist and often made music with the intellectuals she succoured. After 1945 there were successively different waves of refugees from Eastern Europe, the Middle East, South America, South Africa, and other parts of the globe. In her later years Hoffenberg helped facilitate her visit to Oxford for a thanksgiving event to celebrate the life of the biochemist and pharmacologist, Hugh Blaschko who died in 1993.

By 1992 the Society's activities had wound down to such an extent that it was threatened with closure. Hoffenberg proposed a major appeal for funds but Sir Anthony Kenny took a negative view: 'We are no longer able to provide temporary haven for scientists and scholars of international repute ... we are mainly funding comparatively junior academics from Third World countries ...' This view did not however prevail in the Society, and Hoffenberg's appeal was able to generate considerable funds, especially from the Wolfson Foundation. In 1999 the Society, which changed its name to the Council for Assisting Refugee Academics (CARA), was providing grants to 25 scholars from eastern and southern Africa and the Middle East who had lost their jobs as a result of political, racial or religious discrimination.[13] Hoffenberg maintained his involvement as President until 2002 and was especially pro-active in enhancing the provision of English language training.

Allied to support for the refugees is the care of the victims of torture. Hoffenberg was an active patron of the Medical Foundation for the Care of Victims of Torture (see chapter 10) which established a clinic in London. He took part in fundraising receptions in Oxford, helped to facilitate the support of the Wolfson Foundation and promoted educational initiatives designed to keep this issue in the public domain.[14]

The medical consequences of nuclear warfare

Hoffenberg had a long-standing central commitment to publicizing the medical consequences of nuclear war and to promoting international agreement which would limit the expansion of the nuclear arsenal and eventually abolish it. He had emerged in 1945 from the army with pacifist ideas, somewhat tempered over the years, and had been appalled by the dropping of the atom bombs on Japan. He recalled:

> When I heard the news in Italy my immediate reaction was one of elation and relief because it meant we didn't have to go out to the Far East, and it looked as though the war was going to end. But as I began to think about it and got to know Norman Cousins in the States, who had adopted a lot of very badly burned Japanese girls – the Hiroshima maidens – the horror came home.[15]

In 1981 Hoffenberg became a founding member of the Birmingham branch of the Medical Campaign Against Nuclear Weapons and later became its President. At the Faculty of Medicine and Dentistry at Birmingham University in 1983 he sought to organize a seminar on medical problems associated with nuclear warfare. The Faculty expressed reservations about becoming associated with any political pressure group but distinguished the simple use of Faculty facilities. He prevailed on the

Dean, Tom Whitehead, to agree that it would not be impossible to separate the purely medical aspects of nuclear warfare from the wider political debate about nuclear weapons.[16]

The organisation of International Physicians for the Prevention of Nuclear War attracted Hoffenberg's interest – as well as the opprobrium of right-wing journalists who remembered the Nolte affair (see chapter 7). Despite this, Ronald Reagan's message delivered to a meeting of the organisation in 1983 included the following:

> Nuclear war cannot be won and must never be fought. No task has greater significance for us, for our Allies, and for the entire world than to work for the success of the Geneva negotiations to reverse the growth in nuclear arsenals and to move towards genuine peace. These negotiations ... are critically important. They deserve the full support of all, like your organization, who seek genuine progress towards peace.[17]

Hoffenberg's friend, Bernard Lown, noted that 'Advances in weapon technology have spawned a number of illusions, including that of gaining nuclear superiority and entertaining the possibility of victory.' He proposed an addition to the Hippocratic oath 'to include a recognition that nuclear war constituted the greatest contemporary threat to life and health ...' Dr Herbert Abrams suggested that 'A belief in the possibility of victory could be predicated only on an illusion that nuclear war was "survivable"... What, for the individual, must be defined was *acceptable* survival.' Norman Dixon, a professor of psychology, suggested that 'since even the least neurotic, most disinterested, and level headed of people had been known to make decisions of such monstrous proportions that they defied rational explanation, we should consider very carefully what might happen if we entrusted life-or-death decisions to people so lacking insight into the neurotic needs by which they were driven ...' A former commander-in-chief of the US Forces in the Pacific, Admiral Gayler, maintained that nuclear weapons had no sensible military use.

Hoffenberg believed that the risk of nuclear warfare had become infinitely greater since a number of smaller countries had 'a nuclear capability and probably less sense of responsibility'. He was greatly concerned in 1991 by the proposed resumption of UK nuclear tests and wrote:

> We understand that the British government is shortly preparing to explode a nuclear device under the Nevada desert. There is a growing public perception that nuclear weapons are unacceptably dangerous. Even those who believed they served a purpose as a deterrent are beginning to accept that with the collapse of the Soviet Union they are no longer necessary and even counter-productive.
>
> The production of nuclear weapons is fuelled by testing them. Until recently there has been general ignorance of the effects of nuclear testing but

a report, *Radioactive Heaven and Earth*, produced last August by International Physicians for the Prevention of Nuclear War, has made a serious attempt to quantify the consequences.

For example, the authors estimate that the radioactive materials released hitherto by atmospheric testing (now universally abandoned) and incorporated into human beings by the end of this century will eventually produce 430,000 cancer fatalities, some of which have already occurred. Ultimately the total number of cancer fatalities could be as high as 2.4 million.

The authors show that underground testing is leaving behind large quantities of long-lived radioactive materials at test sites around the world, that leakage from these sites is not improbable, and this would pose a threat to future generations.

Nuclear tests are in essence turning the Nevada and other nuclear test sites into huge unstudied and unlicensed nuclear dumps for high-level radioactive waste. At Nevada, for example, there are over 1,700 kilograms of plutonium 239, which has a half-life of 24,400 years.

In view of the growing evidence that nuclear testing is dangerous to both the health of populations and the environment we find it extraordinary that the government still proposes to conduct its test at the Nevada site and call on it to think again.[18]

In 1992 Hoffenberg had crafted an alliance between the Medical Association for the Prevention of War and the Medical Campaign against Nuclear Weapons, which held its first conference at the Royal College of Physicians in London. He continued his activist attacks on the pro-nuclear lobbies. On the possible disappearance of a nuclear threat, he wrote:

> You have to be an optimist. You have to believe a nuclear free world is possible. It's rather like medical researchers. They believe they can solve anything. They're probably not right. But if you don't believe that then you don't do anything. You must believe it's attainable in the end. Sometime or other the world will wake up to it.[19]

Hoffenberg's fearlessness in sometimes pursuing unpopular causes did not help his standing in Establishment circles. He did not go to the House of Lords.

CHAPTER TWELVE

The later years

University of Queensland

After leaving Wolfson College in September 1993, Hoffenberg made his home in Australia. He joined the University of Queensland in Brisbane where he took up a half-time appointment as Professor of Medical Ethics and bought a house at Ascot in the suburbs.

Both his sons had emigrated to Queensland. Derek, the elder, after studying at the Royal Agricultural College, Cirencester, set out to see the world. In 1983 he became a jackeroo at Moree, New South Wales on a property owned by Sinclair Hill, a grazier with a string of properties from New South Wales north to western Queensland. Derek bought a holding in the semi-arid Longreach District in 1986, and married Sinclair Hill's daughter Ayesha in April 1991. They had three children, Sophia, Imogen and Oliver, and the normally restrained Hoffenberg was suitably emotional upon the birth of his first granddaughter. So as to be closer to his parents, in 2001 Derek and Ayesha moved with their young family to Toowoomba, a large country town one and a half hour's drive from Brisbane.

Peter Hoffenberg studied marine geography at Cardiff and went on to the London School of Economics to read for a Masters degree in Marine Law, Economics and Politics. After further postgraduate study at the University of Queensland he worked in Rockhampton at the University of Southern Queensland Centre for Water Resources Development. Peter became much involved in geographical information systems, which led him to senior posts with the Queensland Government; he married Carol McColl and settled at Fig Tree Pocket in Brisbane.[1]

At the University of Queensland Hoffenberg gave few formal lectures in ethics, preferring to teach small groups. He would join hospital consultants and the junior doctors and students who accompanied them on their ward rounds. At the end of the round he would spend an hour discussing any ethical problems associated with the patients' symptoms and treatment. This approach evoked lively student discussion and ethical dilemmas could be illustrated in a 'real' as distinct from a wholly theoretical and philosophical framework.

Margaret with son Derek and granddaughter, Sophia, 1999.

Peter Hoffenberg, 2000.

Hoffenberg also lectured to many community groups on issues of medical ethics and participated in seminars at John Morgan's ethics centre at St John's College. He was much involved in Dr Mal Parker's Ethics Interest Group in the School of Medicine at the University of Queensland, both as a member and a presenter and made significant contributions to the discussions on end-of-life issues and on the ethical aspects of organ transplants. Margaret Steinberg recruited Colleen Cartwright to undertake research on healthy ageing and Hoffenberg became her special mentor. The results of their first survey illuminated community and health profession-als' attitudes to end-of-life issues, where these related to a patient's right to self-determination, pain management, enduring power of attorney and the creation of advance health directives.[2] The group then carried out a further study[3] to develop a protocol for an advance health directive for patients who were terminally ill; Hoffenberg helped considerably in formulating the wording of the questionnaire. Whereas in Queensland patients could yield power of attorney with respect to their management of property, special provisions were needed to allow patients to express their wishes concerning their future treatment and to give effect to this through a trusted person. A Bill to this effect was passed in the last days of the 1998 Queensland Conservative Government.

In later years Hoffenberg took the opportunity to reiterate this increas-ingly strongly held view that doctors owed a special duty of care to patients in the closing phases of life. In 2004 a Bill was introduced into the House of Lords by Lord Joffe entitled 'Assisted Dying for the Terminally Ill'. He made one of the few submissions that were published in which he sought to answer some of the common objections to physicians assisting the death of the terminally ill.[4] However, the Bill was defeated by 140 to 100.

In 1995 the Hoffenbergs returned to live in Britain and bought an apartment in the imposing Sherborne House, set in a rural landscape close to Oxford. However, Hoffenberg found the farm machinery which sometimes blocked the lane to the railway station, coupled with the unre-liability of rail travel, insurmountable impediments to keeping his appointments in London. The Hoffenbergs moved back to Australia in 2000 taking an apartment above the river at Newstead, Brisbane where Peter and Derek and their families were more accessible. From then on, almost every year they made long visits to South Africa.

Return to South Africa

Following the departure of P.W. Botha in 1989, the new leader of South Africa, F.W. de Klerk, had moved away from the previous policies of government violence and repression and 'sought to develop a power base

An evening at the opera. Picnicking on the lawn at Glyndebourne with Margaret, 1995.

and constitutional system, that, while it might end the overall political dominance of whites, would protect their position in the country'. The forecast blood-bath was thus avoided, and black Africans eventually came to power through a negotiated settlement, a process of transition and not revolution. 'The Bill of Rights guaranteed key individual freedoms of expression and of association, recognition of property rights, and a constitutional court to defend them.' The new Government reduced defence spending, increased funding for education, health and social welfare, but followed conservative fiscal policies; many black Africans found their immediate expectations of the New Millennium unrealized.[5]

Despite several requests to do so over the years, the Hoffenbergs had decided not to go back together to visit South Africa until all political exiles were allowed to return. Their first return visit occurred in 1991 when Derek and Ayesha Hoffenberg agreed to join them for a family Christmas. It was an emotional return for the patriot Hoffenberg who had been away from his homeland for nearly 24 years. He now had a British passport and had been obliged to renounce South African citizenship. In the arrival hall of the airport he and Margaret were asked to wait. After about half an hour the immigration official returned with a broad smile on his face: 'Welcome home, Dr Hoffenberg!'[6]

A later working visit took place at the invitation of Hoffenberg's former protégé, Nkosasana Dhlamini. Dhlamini had been a student activist who escaped to Britain during her final year of medical training at the University of Natal. Hoffenberg, whilst at Birmingham , had arranged for her to complete her training at Bristol. She became Minister for Health in Nelson Mandela's 1994 Government of National Unity. She was then married to the Minister, Jacob Zuma, whom she later divorced. On a visit to Oxford she had recruited Hoffenberg and commissioned him to work in the South African Ministry of Health, where he spent six months in 1995–1996

Dhlamini envisaged a reformed health service which would redress some of the inequities of the past. She moved resources towards primary health facilities and community services, such as prenatal and postnatal care and for children under six years. She attempted to build up a network of clinics throughout the country and to address the deficiencies of health care in rural and poorer urban areas. Hoffenberg joined her Advisory Committee and faced a plethora of challenges. He was asked to draft legislation on a number of health issues, including organ transplants and in doing so he made great use of UK healthcare legislation.

Nkosasana sought to establish Academic Health Service Complexes (AHSC) for educating health professionals at all levels. Hoffenberg and Hugh Philpott were asked to investigate and report on the status of academic medicine.[7] Hoffenberg recalled:

When I left South Africa in 1968 academic medicine was flourishing. The standard of teaching and practice was excellent, good quality research was being conducted in all medical schools, morale was high. The best graduates wanted to pursue academic careers and there was fierce competition for posts in teaching hospitals. The picture was not so rosy when one looked more closely at the general medical scene. Very few black doctors were being trained – 7 in 1966, 11 in 1967, 10 in 1968. The distribution of doctors was distorted in favour of white suburbs where a ratio of one per 450 people was not uncommon; in black areas there might be one per 100 000 or even 250,000 people ... This inequality of service was reflected in patterns of health and disease ...

He found in 1995 that the status of academic medicine had declined badly under the Nationalist Government. Teaching hospitals had lost funding, 61 per cent of government health funding went to the private sector and great numbers of doctors had left South Africa. Later Hoffenberg wrote to the London *Times* suggesting that it was immoral for the UK National Health Service to be recruiting doctors from South Africa where it cost £140,000 to train a doctor and where grave shortages existed.[8] Because of the disparity between lucrative private practice and working full-time in the public sector, government salaries had been increased substantially, and 'Limited Private Practice' was permitted out of hours; in the face of evidence that this was being abused, the Advisory Group recommended it be phased out but were defeated by the doctors' fierce opposition.

There was an urgent need to change the pattern of student entry to medicine in order to reflect more equitably the ethnic make-up of South Africa. Although 75 per cent of the population were black African, only 27 per cent of medical students in 1995 were black, whilst the 13 per cent white population provided 51 per cent. The non-whites suffered from inadequate preparation in the schools, and Hoffenberg was pleased to find it was the Afrikaner universities at Bloemfontein and Pretoria which were most successful in providing remedial courses in computer skills and the sciences which led to a successful induction to the medical course. Stellenbosch university used the Afrikaans language for teaching, but successfully trained Coloured students. The government had shown its commitment by building new hospital complexes at Cato Manor outside Durban, and in Umtata in the Eastern Cape.

The latter, located in the University of Transkei, caused Hoffenberg and Philpott most concern. Umtata had been the capital of the Eastern Cape Province, until the capital was moved to Bhisho, close to East London. This was a significant factor that accounted for the advanced state of decay they found at Umtata, where the hospital and medical school buildings were in bad shape, animals roamed the corridors, and there were 66 vacancies out of an establishment of 105 teaching posts. The majority of the mainly expatriate staff had degrees from eastern Europe and other places which, whilst formerly registrable in the Transkei, were unacceptable in South Africa. There were vacant headships for the departments of internal medicine, obstetrics and gynaecology, general surgery, paediatrics, psychiatry and about 10 other disciplines. The Dean had a flourishing private practice in East London, and many of the staff lacked academic commitment. Hoffenberg and Philpott recommended the Medical School be closed until adequate hospital facilities could be built and linkages developed with hospitals in East London and science teaching in Port Elizabeth.

Dhlamini was greatly displeased by their report, and Hoffenberg concluded that any future work under her aegis would be fraught. However, their recommendation that the medical school at the University of Transkei should be closed was firmly endorsed in 2000 by Hoffenberg's good friend, Kader Asmal, Minister for Education (who had trained in England). Dhlamini left the Health portfolio and became Foreign Minister. Hoffenberg encountered many in the Ministry of Health who had been promoted beyond their capability and lacked the experience needed to exercise their role effectively. Sceptical about the benefits of 'affirmative action' in the USA, Hoffenberg believed strongly that a non-racist meritocracy was the best paradigm for the functioning of a welfare state and one which would most assist the disadvantaged – to whose advancement he had a life-long commitment.

Despite the inevitable diversion of funds from universities and urban areas to meet needs which had been previously neglected, Hoffenberg still found an overall high quality amongst the medical academics and the beleaguered research workers who had showed great fortitude in adapting to the new winds of change.[9]

On their first visits back to South Africa the Hoffenbergs were greatly fêted, and became immersed in cocktail parties and dinners in Cape Town and Johannesburg. They were pleased to revive old friendships, but some people who had shunned Hoffenberg when banned now sought the companionship of the distinguished 'Sir Raymond'. A good many of their English-speaking acquaintances had continued a relatively sybaritic existence, unrepentant about their past support for a regime which so disadvantaged black Africans and which disregarded the values of liberal democracy. There were, of course, significant exceptions amongst the English-speaking community, and Hoffenberg was pleased and surprised to find a higher proportion of Afrikaners who sincerely regretted the apartheid years, who would say 'we got it all wrong', and who were seriously working with the ANC to build a truly integrated South Africa.

The Hoffenbergs usually spent the first two or three months of the year in South Africa, but quickly tired of the social round. Margaret had spent

Being gowned by Ralph Kirsch, Head of Department of Medicine at the University of Cape Town following election to the Fellowship, 1999.

some childhood holidays on a farm her father owned near The Wilderness, a small seaside town about 15 kilometres from George, on the southern coast. They often rented a comfortable apartment in Zade's House – a house perched on a dune with a view of the sea, headlands and rocks, and about five kilometres of beach. There were dolphins and whales, and good surf. Hoffenberg had given up fishing when it seemed probable to him that fish might feel pain, but he walked a good deal,

Return to Grey High School, Port Elizabeth, 2001.

144

played golf and read books. They were close to National Parks. It was a quiet, safe part of South Africa, relatively free of the crime and the racial tensions which bedevilled many parts of Natal, Johannesburg and Cape Town. Hoffenberg believed much of the crime in South Africa was socially circumstantial, associated with deprivation, rather than culturally inherent; his great fear was the future impact on society of the AIDS orphans and their poor family circumstances.[10]

In May 2004 Hoffenberg was surprised that Helen Suzman, great campaigner for human rights in South Africa, was reported in the London *Daily Telegraph* as attacking the ANC Government. Hoffenberg's response encapsulated his optimistic assessment more than twelve years after his return to South Africa:

> Since she first entered politics I have had great admiration for Helen Suzman and her brave opposition to apartheid during its darkest years. It is with sadness that I feel obliged to reply ... Her view that 'even apartheid was better' is not likely to be shared by the vast majority of the population who are now free after 40 years of Nationalist Party rule and 350 years of colonial oppression. Her statement that parliamentary democracy was healthier under apartheid borders on the absurd; has she forgotten that over 80% of the population was not represented?
>
> I agree that many of the poorest people in the country have not benefited as much as they might have been led to expect. However, there have been

With Madeleine, 2006.

impressive achievements in the provision of housing, water, electricity and, above all, access to proper education for those who were denied these things under apartheid ... The main accomplishment of the ANC has been to create a politically stable society in which all races live in harmony ...

I believe she misrepresents Mbeki when she attributes 'anti-whitism' to him ... He is determined to show that blacks can and will run a large non-racial modern country efficiently and justly ...

It takes time and resources to reverse the consequences of centuries of suppression.[11]

Hoffenberg also castigated Suzman for her earlier support for Chief Gatsha Buthelezi, which had exacerbated conflict with the ANC.

Margaret Hoffenberg's health deteriorated in 2004; after a series of falls she became bedridden in March 2005 and was nursed at home in Brisbane until her death from cancer on 27 June 2005. Hoffenberg rarely left the apartment during this period. The Hoffenbergs had been a remarkable team during 55 years of marriage. Margaret had shared Bill's commitments, and in November 2004 she expressed the view that their years of struggle against apartheid and her work with the Kupugani organization had been their most meaningful and rewarding period.[12]

Madeleine Douglas, an art consultant, and with a strong interest in medical ethics had been active in the formation of an Institute of Medical Ethics at the University of Bonn and in the development of its links with Oxford where she and Hoffenberg had become acquainted. After the death of his wife, their friendship deepened. In Brisbane he had a major surgical operation for cancer in June 2006 and Madeleine supported him assiduously towards recovery. They married in December 2006, but there was a recurrence of cancer which ended his life. He died in Oxford on 22 April 2007. Madeleine, gifted, empathic, and elegant gave his life a remarkable coda.

There was a splendid celebration of Hoffenberg's life on 17 November 2007 when about 300 people joined with the Royal College of Physicians at Wolfson College, Oxford, for a luncheon with jazz. Professor Jon Stallworth presided and Professor Ian Gilmore, President of the Royal College of Physicians, spoke. He was followed by long and amusing speeches by friends and colleagues who had shared different aspects of Hoffenberg's life: Professor David London from Birmingham and the Royal College, Jonty Driver, originally from the South African student turmoil, and Dr John Penney, his close colleague at Wolfson. In April 2008 the South African Government invested Hoffenberg posthumously with the Order of the Grand Counsellor of the Baobab (Silver) for 'his excellent contribution in the advancement of the medicine field and opposing apartheid policies'.

A Summation of Hoffenberg's Life

Bill Hoffenberg had a private *persona*; his deeper thoughts and motivations must be guessed from his writings and lectures, and his life. There was a certain calm reserve about him which enabled him to dissemble some of his responses and feelings. This contained a paradox: a humility in the face of his high standards for achievement, but also some *hauteur* linked to his stature and sense of self-worth. After all, the superficial evidence of an accumulation of six honorary doctorates and seven fellowships of learned societies indicates he became used to recognition as the norm.[13]

He was a physically impressive man: tall (185 cm), large physique; strong, good features (despite a broken nose), and a graceful stride. Hoffenberg was a superb athlete who excelled at many sports and whose success usually arose more from a determination to execute movements to his standards of precision than from the desire to devastate his opponents. His physical energy enabled him to enjoy many forms of recreation, but more significantly gave him the strength to sustain the commitment which led to the achievement of intellectual and philosophical goals.

Hoffenberg possessed a powerful intellect characterized by a willingness to make lateral associations and bravely to explore bordering disciplines, for example mathematics, if they bore on the problems he attempted to solve. He was an early user of radioisotopes in metabolism and diagnostic therapy, and curious about how the body functions. His research approach was often pragmatic in the first phase; the theoretical basis for understanding biological processes sometimes came later. Hoffenberg had a strong innate scepticism, revealed especially in his public pronouncements which might run counter to scientific fashion. He welcomed the unexpected result but was sceptical of its significance until confirmed; for instance, he was the first to discover that a high level of long-acting thyroid stimulator activity was restricted to the gamma-globulin fraction, but decided to repeat the study before making his result public and was pre-empted in the interim by J.M. McKenzie. His sense of proportion informed his scientific assessments and provided the basis for his sense of humour, which was expressed with wit and some elegance, since he was articulate and had a well-developed control of language. His writing was cogent and lucid.

Hoffenberg's main research achievements concerned the functioning of the thyroid gland; he started his education in this field in Raymond

Greene's laboratory at New End Hospital in 1953 and persisted until at Birmingham University in 1985 he left behind a group of researchers internationally recognized for its excellence. He developed a double radioimmunoassay for the presence of thyroglobulin which was still widely adopted in many countries in 2005; this test was of crucial importance in determining whether patients had a recurrence of thyroid cancer or not. He made many contributions to the development of endocrinology as a discipline. In addressing the Royal Society of Medicine in 1978 he made one of those clarifying statements, the content of which was known to scientists but never explicitly realized. In speaking of hormonal action, he said: 'We now know that what is synthesized by a cell is not necessarily what is secreted by it; what is secreted by a cell is not necessarily what reaches the target [cell] and what reaches the target is not necessarily what acts upon it.'

Hoffenberg made a major contribution to understanding the aetiology of the widespread disease Kwashiorkor, and was able to demonstrate the separate mechanisms controlling albumin synthesis and its breakdown, and to develop a scenario for the metabolism of albumin. His research in the 1950s on persons whose sexual differentiation was ambivalent or rudimentary was pioneering and led both to a better understanding of the intersex and to a superior basis for clinical therapy.

A gifted teacher, Hoffenberg emphasized the exposure of students to clinical experience and its attendant problem-solving, and the development of a good base in hard science. At Birmingham University he was able to bring an additional four hospitals into clinical teaching. Unlike some medical schools whose emphasis was professional rather than scientific, Hoffenberg's Department of Medicine built up postgraduate research education. This was of value to him when he steered the fortunes of Wolfson College, the largest residential postgraduate College in Oxford; he was much at home with its international character. His term as President of the Royal College of Physicians in London was marked by increasing regionalization of its educational activities, as College tutors were appointed and lectures held in rural areas to foster the continuing education of physicians.

During Hoffenberg's six-year Presidency he attempted to reform the standards of medical practice from within. He sought a wider participation in medical audit, greater awareness of medical fraud and misconduct, and more stringent relations between physicians and pharmaceutical companies, coupled with more rigorous standards of scientific publication. The use of volunteers and patients in research was also addressed. His book, *Clinical Freedom*, expounded the need for a different balance between informed patient autonomy, the authority of the physician and the responsibility of government for patient care. Hoffenberg was opposed to defensive medicine, reinvigorated the debate on 'no-fault' medical insurance, and sought better government funding of preventive medicine.

An activist is one who zealously pursues a cause. Hoffenberg spoke up strongly for the reform of the National Health Service, but this was but one of the many causes to which he was committed. The worth of individuals and the need for their self-realization were his basic affirmation and this led him to the non-racist outlook which resulted in his exile from the loved South Africa he had served while at risk during World War II. The boy from provincial Port Elizabeth became the international medical activist. His passion for justice brought him to the Chair of the Defence and Aid Fund which helped black Africans accused of political misdemeanours.

This imperative about justice was balanced by his compassion and empathy with people, so that Hoffenberg was an early carer for the victims of torture and for refugee academics, and an exponent of the medical consequences of testing nuclear weapons. He was much concerned with end-of-life issues, promulgated the death of the brainstem as the criterion for mortality, and believed physicians had a duty of care to ensure the wishes of patients regarding their demise were fulfilled with minimum suffering.

Hoffenberg was for many years in debates directed to increasing the supply of donor organs for transplant; his reasoned value system which placed the needs of the patient at its centre was at issue with the religious fundamentalists who sought to continue ventilating cadavers. The sense of proportion at the heart of his value system is illustrated by an incident when the Queensland racist and populist Pauline Hanson was sent to gaol for a technicality of electoral fraud; the anti-racist Hoffenberg was incensed by this decision.[14]

Hoffenberg believed advances in research should be generated and applied to relieve the suffering of the disadvantaged. This led him to senior positions in a number of charities where his organizational flair was directed to community health: cancer, heart disease, mental illness, the needs of people with physical disabilities and greater support for preventive medicine. His first wife, Margaret, was a great support in all his activities.

Hoffenberg's zest for life, his wit and his conviviality enriched the lives of his family, his friends and his colleagues. He exemplified a person, gifted physically and intellectually, who applied his talents tenaciously as scientist and physician, humanitarian and academic.

Chronology

1923   Birth of Raymond (Bill) Hoffenberg, Port Elizabeth, South Africa, *6 March*

1928   Grey Preparatory School, Port Elizabeth

1929   Grey Junior School, Port Elizabeth

1935   Grey High School, Port Elizabeth

1939   Undergraduate, University of Cape Town Medical School

1942   Enlisted in Army as stretcher bearer. To North Africa

1944   Italian campaign (to 1945)

1946   Demobilisation and resumption of medical course

1948   Graduated MB, ChB

1949   Married Margaret Rosenberg

1951   Medical School, Hammersmith Hospital, UK. Registrar, Endocrine Unit, New End Hospital

1953   MRCP, London

1954   Senior Research Fellow, CSIR, South Africa

1955   Lecturer and Senior Lecturer, Department of Medicine, University of Cape Town and Consultant Physician, Groote Schuur Hospital (to 1967).

1957   Travelling Fellow, Carnegie Corporation and Cecil John Adams Fellow; to USA. MD, University of Cape Town

1965   Chair, South African Defence and Aid Fund (to 1966)

1966   Fellow, University of Cape Town

1967   Banned by South African Government, *28 July*

1968   PhD, University of Cape Town; emigration to UK, *28 March*. Senior Scientist, MRC, Division of Biophysics, National Institute of Medical Research (to 1970) and Consultant Physician (Endocrinology) New End Hospital and Royal Free Hospital Medical School, London

1970   Clinical Research Centre, Harrow (to 1972)

1971   FRCP, London; Editor, *Clinical Science*

1972   William Withering Professor of Medicine, University of Birmingham (to 1985)

1973 Oliver-Sharpey lecture to Royal College of Physicians

1975 Editor, *Quarterly Journal of Medicine*

1976 Executive, International Society for Endocrinology (to 1988)

1977 Procensor and Censor, Royal College of Physicians; Executive, Association of Physicians

1978 Council, Royal Society of Medicine; Chair, Medical Research Society; Medical Research Council

1981 Senior Censor and Vice President, Royal College of Physicians; President, Medical Campaign against Nuclear Weapons

1983 President, Royal College of Physicians, *28 March* (to 1989)

1984 KBE

1985 President, Wolfson College, Oxford (to 1993)

1986 Rock Carling Fellowship 'Clinical Freedom'; Chair, UK Cancer Committee for Coordinating Research (to 1991)

1987 Chair, British Heart Foundation (to 1993); Trustee, Wolfson Foundation (to 1993)

1989 President, Mental Health Foundation; Trustee, Nuffield Provincial Hospitals Trust (to 1993)

1991 First return visit to South Africa, *December*; President, Society for Protection of Science and Learning (to 2002). Harveian Orator, Royal College of Physicians

1993 Professor of Medical Ethics, University of Queensland (to 1995)

1995 Adviser, South African Ministry of Health

1996 Resident at Sherborne House, Sherborne UK (to 2000)

2000 Resident at Newstead, Brisbane

2005 Death of Margaret Hoffenberg, *27 June*

2006 Married Madeleine Douglas, *December*

2007 Death of Raymond Hoffenberg, *22 April*

Notes

Notes on sources

The library of the Royal College of Physicians, London, the archives of Wolfson College, Oxford, and the Special Collections Department of the University of Birmingham Library are the main source of material, augmented by family papers held by the Hoffenberg family, including a personal unpublished memoir which is cited in these Notes as 'RH autobiography'. The author holds letters and records from many people who knew Hoffenberg, and other sources are mentioned in the acknowledgements at the beginning of the monograph.

Abbreviations

HFP	Hoffenberg Family Papers
IFTE	International Forum for Transplant Ethics
LRH	L.R. Humphreys
RCP	Royal College of Physicians, London, Archives
RH	Sir Raymond (Bill) Hoffenberg
UBSC	University of Birmingham Special Collections
WCA	Wolfson College Archives

Chapter 1: Port Elizabeth

1   L. Marquard, *The Peoples and Policies of South Africa*, Oxford University Press, Cape Town, 1960, p.8; D. Tutu, *No Future Without Forgiveness*, Rider, London, 1999, p.87.

2   RH to LRH, 28 August and 16 December 2004; HFP, RH autobiography, pp.1–4.

Chapter 2: A lance corporal in North Africa and Italy

1   RH to LRH, 19 November 2004; HFP; RH autobiography, pp.4–8.

2   V. Alhadeff, *South Africa in Two World Wars*, Don Nelson, 1979, Cape Town, pp.101, 105.

3   G.A. Shepperd, *The Italian Campaign 1943–45: A Political and Military Reassessment*, Arthur Barker, 1968, London, pp.199, 256.

4   Alhadeff, p.108; Shepperd, pp.255, 276; RH to LRH, 19 November 2004.

5   Alhadeff, pp.110, 112; Shepperd, p.292; HFP, RH autobiography, pp.8–9.

6   Alhadeff, pp.112–115; Shepperd, pp.x, 314.
7   HFP, RH autobiography, pp.9–10.
8   C.J.C. Molony, *History of the Second World War, The Mediterranean and the Middle East, Volume VI*, HMSO, London, 1984, p.256; B. Harpur, *The Impossible Victory*, William Kember, London, 1980, pp.161,179; Shepperd, p.365.
9   HFP, RH autobiography, pp.10–11.

Chapter 3: A physician's focus on research

1   RH to LRH, 15 December 2003 and 19 November 2004; HFP, RH autobiography, p.11–12.
2   RH to LRH, 3 December 2004.
3   RH to LRH, 7 August 2003 and 7 May 2004; RCP, D. Pyke, *Pyke's Notes*, Royal College of Physicians, London, entry for 1988.
4   HFB, RH autobiography, p.10; RH to LRH, 1 November 2004.
5   RH and W.P.U. Jackson 'The problem of intersex', *South African Medical Journal*, 5 May 1956, pp.417–422.
6   W.P.U. Jackson and RH, 'Sex reversal: females with male nuclear sex', Memoir No. 7 of the Society for Endocrinology, 1960, pp.154–161.
7   RH, 'Chromosomes and sex', Proceedings of 43rd South African Medical Congress, 1961, pp.18–24.
8   RH and W.P.U. Jackson, 'Sex chromatin and intersex', *The Journal of Clinical Endocrinology and Metabolism*, vol. 17, 1957, pp.454–458; W.P.U. Jackson and RH, 'Sex reversal: females with male nuclear sex', Memoir No. 7 of the Society for Endocrinology, 1960, pp.154–161.
9   W.P.U. Jackson and RH, 'Turner's syndrome in the male', *South African Medical Journal*, vol. 31, 9 March 1957, pp.226–228.
10 RH and W.P.U. Jackson, 'Gonadal dysgenesis in normal-looking females. A genetic theory to explain variability of the syndrome', *British Medical Journal*, vol. I, 1 June 1957, pp.1281–1284; RH, 'Gonadal dysgenesis: modern concepts', *British Medical Journal*, vol. ii, 21 December 1957, pp.1457–1462.
11 Ibid.; RH to LRH, 29 November 2004.
12 RH to LRH, 7 May 2004.
13 Ibid.
14 RH to LRH, 3 December 2004; HFP, RH, 'Albert Schweitzer'.
15 RH, S. Saunders, G.C. Linder, E. Black and J.F. Brock, 'I[131]-albumin metabolism in human adults after experimental protein depletion and repletion', in *Protein Metabolism*, Springer-Verlag, Berlin, 1962, pp.314–322; RH, E. Black and J.F. Brock, 'Albumin and r-globulin studies in protein depletion states', *Journal of Clinical Investigation*, vol. 45, 1966, pp.143–152.
16 R. Kirsch, L. Frith, E. Black and RH, 'Regulation of albumin synthesis and catabolism by alteration of dietary protein', *Nature*, vol. 217, 10 February 1968, pp.578–579.

[17]   RH, F. Harris and E.G. Black, 'A study of human rickets using Ca-47', Technical Report Series No. 10, International Atomic Energy Agency, Vienna, 1962, pp.85–91.

[18]   F. Harris, RH and E. Black, 'Calcium kinetics in vitamin D deficiency rickets II. Intestinal handling of calcium', *Metabolism*, vol. 14, 1965, pp.1112–1121.

[19]   F. Harris, RH and E. Black, 'Calcium kinetics in vitamin D deficiency rickets I. Plasma kinetic studies after intervenous and oral Ca[47]', *Metabolism*, vol. 14, 1965, pp.1110–1111; F. Harris, RH and E.G. Black, 'The radio-isotope in rickets', *Clinical Science*, vol. 28, 1965, pp.75–82.

[20]   HFP, RH autobiography, p.15.

[21]   RH, 'The thyroid and Osler', *Journal of the Royal College of Physicians*, vol. 19, 1985, pp.50–54; B. Hetzel, 'Iodine deficiency', *ABC Science*, Sydney, 4 June 2001.

[22]   RH, 'Aetiology of hyperthyroidism' – I and II, *British Medical Journal*, vol. 3, 17 and 24 August 1974, pp.452–456, 508–510.

[23]   RH, 'Thyroid function', in *Chemical Diagnosis of Disease*, ed. S.S. Brown, F.L. Mitchell and D.S. Young, Elsevier, 1979, Amsterdam, pp.736–769; D.K. Granner, 'Thyroid hormones', in *Harper's Biochemistry*, ed. R.K. Murray, D.K. Granner, P.A. Mayes and V.W. Rodwell, McGraw-Hill, 2000, New York, pp.561–566.

[24]   RH, 'The eye-signs associated with thyroid disease', *South African Medical Journal*, 26 November 1955, p.1124; RH and L. Eales, 'Chronic thyrotoxic myopathy', *South African Medical Journal*, vol. 30, 1956, pp.1246–1249.

[25]   RH, J.H. Loun and T.J. Voss, 'Thyroidectomy under hypothermia in a pregnant patient with thyroid crisis', *The Lancet*, 23 September 1961, pp.687–689; A.I. Vinik, B.L. Pimstone and RH, 'Sympathetic nervous system blocking in hyperthyroidism', *Journal of Clinical Endocrinology*, vol. 28, 1968, pp.725–727; K. Sterling and RH, 'Beta blocking agents and antithyroid drugs as adjuncts to radioiodine therapy', *Seminars in Nuclear Medicine*, vol. 1, 1971, pp.422–431.

[26]   RH to LRH, 13 October 2004; B.L. Pimstone, RH, and E. Black, 'Parallel assays of thyrotrophin, long-acting thyroid stimulator, and exophthalmos-producing substance in some endocrine disorders', *Journal of Clinical Endocrinology*, vol. 23, 1963, pp.336–345; RH and W.P.V. Jackson, 'Adrenocortical steroids in malignant exophthalmos', *The Lancet*, 29 March 1958, pp.693–695.

[27]   RH, L.R. Purves and E.G. Black, 'The nature of thyroid-stimulating hormones', National Conference on Nuclear Energy 1963: Application of Isotopes and Radiation, 1963, Pretoria, pp.218–225.

[28]   RH and B.L. Pimstone, 'An evaluation of the triiodothyromine suppression test in the diagnosis of hyperthyroidism', National Conference on Nuclear Energy 1963: Application of Isotopes and Radiation, 1963, Pretoria, pp.242–250.

29 A.I. Vinik, B.L. Pimstone and RH, 'Studies on raised free fatty acids in hyperthyroidism', *Metabolism*, vol. 19, 1970, pp.93–101; Shepstone to LRH, 17 October 2003.

30 RH, 'Thyroid stimulating hormones in man', *The Leech*, vol. 34, 1964, pp.134–141.

31 RH to LRH, 8 April and 28 May 2004.

32 RH, 'Triiodothyronine', *Clinical Endocrinology*, vol. 2, 1973, pp.75–87; F.J.R. Hird and V. Trikojus, 'Paper partition chromatography with thyroxine and analogues', *Australian Journal of Science*, vol. 10, 1948, pp.185–187; LRH, *Trikojus: A Scientist for Interesting Times*, Miegunyah Press, 2004, Melbourne, pp.90–93; A.J. Hulbert, 'Thyroid hormones and their effects: a new perspective', *Biological Reviews*, vol. 75, 2000, p.520.

33 D.B. Ramsden and RH, 'Kinetics of the peripheral metabolism of thyroid hormones', in *Quantitative Approaches to Metabolism*, ed. D.G. Gramp, John Wiley & Sons, 1982, New York, pp.301–328; W.A. Burr, E.G. Black, R.S. Griffiths, RH K. Meinhold and K.W. Wenzel, 'Serum triiodothyronine and reverse triiodothyronine concentrations after surgical operation', *The Lancet*, vol. I, 27 December 1975, pp.1277–1279; R.S. Griffiths, E.G. Black and RH, 'Measurement of serum, 3, 3^1, 5^1 – (reverse) T3, with comments on its derivation', *Clinical Endocrinology*, vol. 5, 1976, pp.679–685; Ramsden to LRH, 13 November 2003.

34 RH, 'Peripheral metabolism of hormones: clinical implications', *Journal of the Royal Society of Medicine*, vol. 72, 1979, pp.400–408; A.R. Bradwell, D. Burnett, D.B. Ramsden, W.A. Burr, H.P. Prince and RH, 'Preparation of a monospecific antiserum to thyroxine binding globulin for its quantitation by rocket immunoelectrophoresis', *Clinica Chimica Acta*, vol. 71, 1976, pp.50–510.

35 RH and D.B. Ramsden, 'The transport of thyroid hormones', *Clinical Science*, vol. 65, 1983, pp.337–342; D.B. Ramsden and RH, 'The actions of thyroid hormones mediated via the cell nucleus and their clinical significance', *Clinics in Endocrinology and Metabolism*, vol. 12, 1983, pp.101–115.

36 A.Y. Al-Hindawi, E.G. Black, D.B. Brewer, S.G. Griffits and RH, 'Measurement of thyroid hormone in experimental thyroid tumours in rats', *Journal of Endocrinology*, vol. 75, 1977, pp.245–250; RH, 'Radiation-induced thyroid tumours in man: discussion paper', *Journal of the Royal Society of Medicine*, vol. 75, 1982, pp.893–896.

37 RH, 'The present role of *in vitro* tests of thyroid function', *Journal of Clinical Pathology*, vol. 28, 1975, pp.239–243.

38 M.N. Moreira-Andres, E.G. Black, D.B. Ramsden and RH, 'The effect of calorie restrictions on serum thyroid hormone binding proteins and free hormone in obese patients', *Clinical Endocrinology*, vol. 12, 1980, pp.249–255.

39   Franklyn to LRH, 4 November 2003; J.A. Franklyn, 'Free triiodothyronine and free thyroxine in sera of pregnant women and subjects with congenitally increased or decreased thyroxine-binding globulin', *Clinical Chemistry*, vol. 29, 1983, pp.1527–1530.
40   P.M. Jefferys, RH, H.E.A. Farran, P.M. Fraser and H.M. Hodgkinson, 'Thyroid-function tests in the elderly', *The Lancet*, 29 April 1972, pp.924–927.
41   E.G. Black, S.J. Bodden, J.A. Hulse and RH, 'Serum thyroglobulin in normal and hypothyroid neonates', *Clinical Endocrinology*, vol. 16, 1982, pp.267–274.
42   E.G. Black, A. Cassoni, T.M.D. Gimlette, C.L. Harmer, M.N. Maisey, G.D. Oates, 'Serum thyroglobulin in thyroid cancer', *The Lancet*, 29 August 1981, pp.443–445; E.G. Black and RH, 'Should one measure serum thyroglobulin in the presence of anti-thyroglobulin antibodies?', *Clinical Endocrinology*, vol. 18, 1983, pp.597–601; D.S. Fairweather, A.R. Boadwell, S.F. Watson-James, P.W. Dykes, S. Chanceller and RH, 'Detection of thyroid tumours using radio-labelled anti-thyroglobulin', *Clinical Endocrinology*, vol. 18, 1983, pp.563–570; M.C. Sheppard to LRH, 26 September 2003.

Chapter 4: Human rights in South Africa

1   J. Robertson, *Liberalism in South Africa 1948–1963*, Clarendon Press, Oxford, 1971, p.113.
2   L. Marquard, *The Peoples and Policies of South Africa*, Oxford University Press, Cape Town, 2nd Edition, 1960, pp.26–77; M. Ballinger, *From Union to Apartheid, A Trek to Isolation*, Juta, Cape Town, 1969, pp.17, 226.
3   Marquard, pp.235–6.
4   Ibid., p.151.
5   W. Beinart, *Twentieth-Century South Africa*, Oxford University Press, Oxford, 2001, pp.170–227.
6   Marquard, pp.124–5.
7   Beinart, pp.149–50; Ballinger, pp.259–271, 296–309; H. Suzman, *In No Uncertain Terms*, Alfred Knopf, New York, 1993.
8   Beinart, p.158; Marquard, pp.187–192.
9   Ibid., pp.219, 68; personal communication to LRH, Pietermaritzburg, September 1960.
10   Suzman, pp.31 et seq.
11   RH to LRH, 22 July 2005.
12   Robertson, p.112; Ballinger, pp.402–4; R. Vigne, *Liberals Against Apartheid*, Macmillan Press, Basingstoke, UK, 1997, p.20.
13   Robertson, p.197.
14   Vigne, p.114.
15   Robertson, p.205.
16   RH to LRH, 22 and 9 July 2005.
17   Johannesburg *Sunday Times*, 23 February 1964; *Cape Times*, 24 March 1964.

18 RH, 'Non-white doctors in South Africa', *British Medical Journal*, 28 April 1962, pp.1202–3.

19 T.E.W. Schumann, *The Argus*, 22 February 1963; 'Universities and the community in South Africa', *Nature*, 23 March 1963, pp.1139–1140; RH, 'Science and apartheid', *Nature*, 23 March 1963, p.1141.

20 RH, *The Cape Times*, 31 August 1964.

21 Vigne, p.215; RH to LRH, 22 July 2005.

22 RH to LRH, 9 and 29 July 2005; A. Durbach, *Upington*, Allen & Unwin, St Leonards, Australia, 1999, pp.8–9.

23 Robertson, pp.209, 219–220; Vigne, p.153; RH to LRH, 29 July 2005.

24 M. Gunther, 'The National Committee of Liberation (NCL)/African Resistance Movement (ARM)', in *The Road to Democracy in South Africa*, Volume 1 (1960–1970), Zebra Press, Cape Town, 2004, p.211.

25 Ibid., pp.227–228.

26 Ibid., pp.213, 225, 249–250.

27 Vigne, p.188; RH to LRH, 29 July 2005.

28 Vigne, pp.203–204; RH to LRH, 22 July and 5 August 2005; C.J. Driver, 'Used to be great friends', *Granta* 80, Winter 2002, pp.9–11.

29 HFP, RH to King, 8 April and 29 June 1965.

30 HFP, Jean Hill to Defence and Aid, Cape Town, 31 August and 25 September 1965.

31 RH to LRH, 22 July 2005.

32 RH to LRH, 29 July 2005; Supreme Court of South Africa (Cape of Good Hope Provincial Division), P.1.286/66.

33 Robertson, p.224; Vigne, pp.189–190.

34 Vigne, p.222; Robertson, pp.230–231.

Chapter 5: Hoffenberg banned

1 Directorate of Security Legislation, Security File – Dr Raymond Hoffenberg, File 2/1/1716 of Commissioner, South African Police.

2 *Cape Argus*, 2 January 1968; *Cape Argus*, 1 August 1967; *The Star*, 31 July 1967; *Cape Times*, 5 August 1967; *Sunday Times*, 6 August 1967.

3 *Star*, 25 August 1967; *Rand Daily Mail*, 2 August 1967; *Evening Post*, Port Elizabeth, 26 August 1967; *Cape Argus*, 7 August 1967.

4 *Cape Argus*, 31 July 1967; *Evening Post*, 31 July 1967; *Sunday Times*, 6 August 1967; *Evening Post*, 2 August 1967; *Cape Times*, 12 August 1967; *Cape Times*, 28 August 1967; *Sunday Times*, 27 August 1967; *Rand Daily Mail*, 11 October 1967; *Sunday Times*, 24 September 1967; RH to LRH, 29 July 2005.

5 *Cape Times*, 21 November 1967; *Sunday Times*, 5 November and 6 August 1967.

6 *Rand Daily Mail*, 12 September 1967; *Cape Times*, 2 and 3 November 1967.

7 *Cape Times*, 17 August 1967; *Baltimore Sun*, 24 August 1967; *Progress*, September 1967; *Cape Times*, 29 September 1967; *The Times* (London), 18 August 1967.

8   *Sunday Times*, 13 August 1967; *Cape Times*, 14 August 1967 and
    28 March 1968; *Star*, 2 August 1967; *Cape Argus*, 8 December 1967.
9   *Rand Daily Mail*, 16 August 1967; *Sunday Times*, 1 October 1967.
10 *Sunday Times*, 26 November 1967; *The Times* (London), 9, 12, 16 and
    18 August 1967; *British Medical Journal*, 26 August 1967; *Cape Times*,
    30 August 1967.
11 *Cape Times*, 3 August 1967; RH to LRH, 29 July 2005.
12 *Sunday Times*, 26 November 1967; *Evening Post*, 2 August 1967; *Cape
    Times*, 21 August 1967; *Cape Times*, 15 November 1967.
13 *Sunday Times*, 15 October 1967; *Cape Argus*, 19 October 1967.
14 Directorate of Security Legislation, Security File – Dr Raymond
    Hoffenberg, File 2/1/1716 of Commissioner, South African Police.
15 RH to LRH, 29 July 2005.
16 Ibid.
17 *Cape Argus*, 2 November 1967; *Cape Times*, 4 November and
    15 December 1967; *Cape Argus*, 17 November 1967; *Cape Times*,
    15 December 1967.
18 *Sunday Times*, 1 October 1967; *British Medical Journal*, 7 October 1967;
    Rand Daily Mail, 3 January 1968; RH to LRH, 29 July 2005.
19 *Rand Daily Mail*, 8 February 1968.
20 *Cape Times*, 29 March 1968.
21 RH to LRH, 5 August 2005.

Chapter 6: Birmingham
1   UBSC, Minutes of Faculty of Medicine and Dentistry, 3 July and
    9 October 1972; Wade to LRH, 12 November 2003; RH to LRH,
    27 September 2004.
2   RH to LRH, 7 May 2004: Ramsden to LRH, 13 November 2003;
    Sheppard to LRH, 26 September 2003.
3   RH, '*Tria juncta in uno*: the role of the academic medical unit', Inaugural
    lecture, University of Birmingham, May 1974.
4   Ann Cowell to LRH, 11 November 2003; Elizabeth Black to LRH,
    13 November 2003.
5   D.A. Heath, R. Hoffenberg, J.M. Bishop, M.J. Kendall and O.L. Wade,
    'Medical audits', *Journal of the Royal College of Physicians of London*,
    14, 1980, pp.200–201.
6   RH, *Clinical Freedom*, Nuffield Provincial Hospitals Trust, London, 1987,
    pp.89–96; O.L. Wade, *When I Dropped The Knife*, Pentland Press,
    Durham, 1996, pp.136–7; RH to LRH, 12 July 2004.
7   UBSC, Minutes of Faculty of Medicine and Dentistry, 2 July and
    19 November 1973; 21 January, 6 May and 2 July 1974; Jayne Franklyn
    to LRH, 4 November 2003; M.C. Sheppard to LRH, 26 September 2003;
    RH to LRH, 28 May 2004.
8   UBSC, Minutes of Faculty of Medicine and Dentistry, 21 January and
    9 June 1980; 19 January 1981.

⁹ Elizabeth Black to LRH, 13 November 2003; RH to LRH, 28 May and 1 July 2004; UBSC, Minutes of Faculty of Medicine and Dentistry, 20 November 1972; 20 January 1975; 2 May 1978; 21 November 1983.

¹⁰ Ibid., 17 November 1975; 23 February 1976; 9 May 1977; RH to LRH, 1 July 2004.

¹¹ M.C. Sheppard to LRH, 26 September 2003; RH to LRH, 12 August 2003; 8 May and 27 September 2004; M.W. Makgoba, *Mokoko: The Makgoba Affair*, Vivlia, 1997, Florida Hills, USA, pp.40–41.

Chapter 7: Wolfson College, Oxford

¹ F. Jessup, S. McKerrow and J. Potter, '*Wolfson College Oxford: A Short History*', Wolfson College, Oxford, 1999.

² *College Record 1984–85*, Wolfson College, Oxford, 1985.

³ W. J. Kennedy to LRH, 15 October 2003; Shepstone to LRH, 17 October 2003.

⁴ RH to LRH, 10 July 2003.

⁵ UBSC, Faculty of Medicine and Dentistry, 28 February 1985.

⁶ N. J. Allen to LRH, 22 October 2003.

⁷ M. J. O. Francis to LRH, 20 October 2003.

⁸ RH, 'First Impressions', *Lycidas*, Wolfson College, Oxford, No. 13, 1986, p.2.

⁹ David Ramsden to LRH, 13 November 2003.

¹⁰ J. H. Stallworthy to LRH, 17 October 2003.

¹¹ WCA, G.P.C. 79.6, Investments Working Party Report; G.M. 86.12, 26 November 1986; RH to LRH, 10 July 2003; D. Wyatt to LRH, 20 October 2003.

¹² RH, 'First Impressions', *Lycidas*, Wolfson College, Oxford, No. 13, 1986, p.2.

¹³ J. H. W. Penney to LRH, 17 October 2003; W. J. Kennedy to LRH, 15 October 2003.

¹⁴ RH to LRH, 10 July 2003.

¹⁵ Ibid.; Walton to LRH, 15 October 2003; *Oxford Mail*, 27 September 1988; *Oxford Times*, 23 September 1988; *Daily Telegraph*, 21 September 1988; *The Times*, 28 September 1988; Kennedy to LRH, 15 October 2003; Alan Gordon to LRH, 20 October 2003.

¹⁶ RH, 'Modern medicine: prospects and problems', in *New Prospects for Medicine* (ed. J. M. Austyn), Oxford University Press, Oxford, 1988, pp.8–22.

¹⁷ WCA, Governing Body Minutes, 22 October 1990, 8 May, 5 November and 4 December 1991.

¹⁸ WCA, Governing Body Minutes, 26 October 1988.

¹⁹ College Record, 1987–88, pp.26–7; 1988–89, pp.18–19; 1989–90, pp.21–2; 1990–91, pp.26–27; 1991–92, pp.21–2.

²⁰ K. Forsyth, 'Art 25', *Romulus*, Wolfson College, Oxford, 2 (4), September 1990, pp.3–5.

21 WCA, undated statement by RH; Minutes.
22 WCA, Almond statement of 26 October 1988; Nolte to Almond, 26 June 1988.
23 S. Berger, 'Historians and nation-building in Germany after re-unification', *Past and Present*, No. 148, 1995, pp.187–222.
24 N. Kampe, 'Normalizing the Holocuast? The recent historians' debate in the Federal Republic of Germany', *Holocaust and Genocide Studies*, 2, 1987, pp.61–80.
25 E. Nolte, 'Between myth and revisionism? The Third Reich in the perspective of the 1980s', in *Aspects of the Third Reich*, ed. H. W. Koch, London, 1988, pp.17–38.
26 R. J. Evans, 'The new nationalism and the old history: perspectives on the West German *Historikerstreit*', *Journal of Modern History*, 59, 1987, pp.761–797.
27 Berger, p.210.
28 Kampe, p.67.
29 Evans, p.767.
30 M. Carter, *Anthony Blunt: His Lives*, Pan Macmillan, London, 2001, p.141.
31 WCA, RH to Almond, 25 July 1988; Almond to Nolte, 11 August 1988; Academic Planning Committee, Minutes 3 October 1988.
32 WCA, Minutes of General Meeting, 19 October 1988; *Sunday Telegraph*, 23 October 1988; *Sunday Times*, 6 November 1988; *The Times* (London), 18 October 1985; RH to LRH, 20 November 2003; *Telegraph*, 17 December 1988.
33 *The Observer*, 13 November 1988; *The Independent*, 5 October 1988; *Oxford Times*, 2 December 1988; *Sunday Telegraph*, 30 October 1988.
34 WCA; Roberts to RH, 2 November 1988.
35 *Oxford Times*, 4 November 1988; *The Independent*, 5 November 1988; *Sunday Telegraph*, 6 November 1988; *The Independent*, 5 November 1988.
36 R. L. Hall to LRH, 23 December 2003; Brus to LRH, 14 October 2003; Julian Roberts to LRH, 21 October 2003; *The Independent*, 7 November 1988, WCA, Minutes of Governing Body, 26 October 1988; RH to Goodman, 5 and 10 January 1989; RH to LRH, 10 July 2003.
37 Francis to LRH, 20 October 2003; WCA, Minutes of Governing Body, 21 November 1988 and 18 January 1989; Minutes of General Meeting, 23 November 1988; RH to LRH, 10 July 2003; *The Spectator*, 7 January 1999.
38 *The Spectator*, 17 December 1988; WCA, Minutes of General Purpose Committee, 89/17; C. H. Walton to LRH, 21 October 2003.
39 WCA, Minutes of Fellowship and Membership Committee, 78.20A; Dirk Moses to LRH, 22 October 2003.
40 *Sunday Telegraph*, 19 February 1989; RH to LRH, 20 November 2003.
41 WCA, *College Record*, 1984–85, 1993–94.

42   J. H. W. Penney to LRH, 17 October 2003.
43   WCA, RH, 'Running Wolfson', *Romulus* 2 (2), 1990, p.15; UBSC, Faculty
      Minutes, 4 May 1973; RH to LRH, 10 July 2003, WCA, Governing Body
      Minutes, 30 June 1989; Walton to LRH, 15 October 2003; S. J. Woodell
      to LRH, 21 October 2003.
44   WCA, Governing Body Minutes, 11 March and 11 May 1987; RH to
      LRH, 25 July 2003; S. J. Woodell to LRH, 21 October 2003; P. Kanowski
      to LRH, 20 December 2003.
45   WCA, Governing Body Minutes, 31 May 1990; G. R. Booker to LRH,
      13 October 2003.
46   WCA, College Record 1985–86 President's Letter.
47   WCA, Governing Body Minutes, 30 October 1985, 18 June and
      3 December 1986; G. R. Booker to LRH, 13 October 2003.
48   WCA, Governing Body Minutes, 13 May 1987; 11 May 1988 and
      8 March 1989; C. H. Walton to LRH, 13 October 2003.
49   WCA, Governing Body Minutes, 28 October 1987 and 16 June 1993;
      RH, President's Letter 1992–93, pp.11–12.
50   WCA, Governing Body Minutes, 12 March 1986, 15 June 1988, and
      7 March 1990; *The Times*, 17 May 1990.
51   RH to LRH, 20 November 2003; WCA, Governing Body Minutes,
      15 June 1988, 16 March 1990, 30 January, 8 May, and 4 December 1991,
      11 June 1992.
52   RH to LRH, 10 July 2003; WCA, Centre for Modern Chinese Studies
      Minutes, 4 February 1993; Southwood letter of 28 August 1992; RH to
      Secretary of Faculties, 8 February 1993; Governing Body Minutes,
      28 October and 2 December 1992.
53   WCA, Governing Body Minutes, 4 February and 28 October 1987,
      9 March, 11 May and 26 October 1988, 22 February 1990.
54   Ibid., 16 March 1990, 1 March, 8 May, 30 October, and 4 December
      1991, 11 March 1992, 3 February 1993.
55   Ibid., 17 January 1992; Sue Hales to LRH, 16 October 2003.
56   RH 'Live and Let Die', Valedictory Lecture delivered at Wolfson College,
      June 1993.
57   WCA, Governing Body Minutes, 13 May 1992, 12 May and 16 June 1993.
58   R. J. Roberts to LRH, 20 October 2003; G. R. Booker to LRH,
      13 October 2003; J. H. Stallworthy to LRH, 17 October 2003; WCA,
      College Record 1990–1991, President's Letter, pp.10–11.

Chapter 8: Maintaining standards of medical practice

1   RH, *The Science and Cunning of Physick*: Physicians, Patients and Politics
     in the 1990s, the Harveian Oration, Royal College of Physicians, London,
     1991.
2   RH to LRH, 25 July 2003; D. Pyke, *Pyke's Notes*, Royal College of
     Physicians, London, 1992, entry for 1988; RCP, *Comitia* Minutes,
     28 March 1983.

3   R. Mahler to LRH, 18 September 2003; RCP, D. Pyke, *Pyke's Notes*, p.xii.
4   HFP, Gelfand to RH, 5 April 1983; *Weekend Argus*, 2 April 1983.
5   R. Mahler to LRH, 18 September 2003; RCP, D. Pyke, *Pyke's Notes*, Introduction, 1987 and 1989.
6   Ann Cowell to LRH, 11 November 2003; Michael Tibbs to LRH, 10 November 2003; Bernard Lloyd to LRH, 27 October 2003; *British Medical Journal*, 288, 23 June 1984, p.1922; Batten to LRH, 4 November 2003.
7. RCP, Annual Report, 1988; RH to LRH, 7 and 12 August 2003; H.P. Lambert to LRH, 5 November 2003; Sir Christopher Booth to LRH, 4 November 2003; RCP, RH, 'Annual Address', 16 April 1984.
8   RCP, Bye Law 82; RH to LRH, 2 December 2002; RCP, D. Pyke, *Pyke's Notes*, 1987.
9   RCP Minutes of Council, 12 June 1986, 17 December 1987 and 8 December 1988; RH Annual Address, 13 April 1987, Mahler to LRH, 18 December 2003.
10 RH to LRH, 2 December 2003; RCP, 1989 Annual Report; Minutes of Council, 17 September 1987 and 8 December 1988.
11 RH, 'Medical education for the next century: are we on the right path?', *Newsletter Address to Conversation*, University of Bristol, 1993, 23 (10).
12 RCP, Minutes of Council, 8 September 1988; The Academic Medicine Group, 'Academic medicine: problems and solutions', *British Medical Journal*, 298, 1989, pp.573–9.
13 RH, 'The Science and Currency of Physick'.
14 HFP, RH, 'Back to basics – George Whitfield lecture', University of Birmingham, 8 November 1996; RH, *Clinical Freedom*, pp.41–6, 63–5, 72.
15 HFP, RH, 'Serving two masters', Royal Australian Army Medical Corps, Defence Centre, Brisbane, 11 November 1994.
16 O. Wade, *When I Dropped the Knife*, Pentland Press, Durham, 1966, pp.136–7; RH, *Clinical Freedom*, Nuffield Provincial Hospitals Trust, London, 1987, pp.89–96.
17 RCP, 1989 Annual Report; RCP, *Medical Audit. A First Report. What, Why and How?*, March 1989; Minutes of Council, 8 September and 8 December 1988.
18 Report of a Working Party, *The Relationship between Physicians and the Pharmaceutical Industry*, Royal College of Physicians, London, 1986; N.L. Tilney, R.D. Guttman, A.S. Daar, RH, I. Kennedy, M. Lock, J. Radcliffe-Richards and R.A. Sells, for the International Forum for Transplant Ethics, 'The New Chimera: the industrialization of organ transplantation', *Transplantation*, 71, 2001, pp.591–3.
19 Report of a Working Party, *Fraud and Misconduct in Medical Research*, Royal College of Physicians, London, 1991; HFP, RH, 'Cooking the books: Fraud and misconduct in medicine and science', St John's College, University of Queensland, 2003.
20 RH, *Clinical Freedom*, p.50; RH to LRH, 12 August 2003.

21 British Medical Association, *Report of the Working Party on No-Fault Compensation for Medical Injury*, BMA, London, 1983; Report of a Working Party, *Compensation for Adverse Consequences of Medical Intervention*, Royal College of Physicians, London, 1990; RH, *Clinical Freedom*, pp.81–4.

Chapter 9: The delivery of health services
1   RH, I.P. Todd and G. Pinker, 'Joint statement', *The Lancet*, 12 December 1987.
2   *The Times*, 7 and 14 December 1987; *The Guardian*, 14 December 1987.
3   *The Times*, 10 December 1987; *Sunday Times*, 13 December 1987; RH to LRH, 12 July 2004; *The Independent*, 18 January 1988; *The Telegraph*, 21 January 1988.
4   *The Times*, 21 January 1988; *The Independent*, 21 January 1988.
5   RH to LRH, 17 March 2003 and 12 July 2004.
6   RCP, Minutes of Council, 9 March 1989; 1989 Annual Report; RH to LRH, 12 July 2004; RH, *The Science and Cunning of Physick*, The Harveian Oration, Royal College of Physicians, London, 1991; RH, *Journal of Management in Medicine*, 4, 1989, pp.108–113; *The Times*, 4, 5 and 8 August 1994.
7   RCP, 1984 Annals p.67; 1985 Annual Report; *The Times*, 17 December 1984; RH to LRH, 7 August and 2 December 2003; R. Mahler to LRH, 18 September 2003.
8   *The Times*, 10 August 1983; RCP 1983 Annals, pp.60, 70; RH, 'Modern Medicine: prospects and problems' in *New Prospects for Medicine*, ed. J.M. Austin, Oxford University Press, Oxford, 1988, pp.8–22.
9   RH to LRH, 12 August 2003.
10 RH, *Clinical Freedom*, The Nuffield Provincial Hospitals Trust, London, 1987, pp.13, 18, 25–26, 32, 35; J. Cubbon, 'The Principle of QALY maximisation as the basis for allocating health care resources', *Journal of Medical Ethics*, 17, 1991, 181–184.
11 Report of a Working Party, *Recruitment and Training of Doctors: The Prison Medical Service in England*, Home Office and Department of Health, London, 1990; Margaret Turner-Warwick to LRH, 4 October 2003.
12 RCP, RH, Annual Address, 16 April 1984.
13 RH, *The Science and Cunning of Physick*; Royal College of Physicians, *A Great and Growing Evil: The Medical Consequences of Alcohol Abuse*, Tavistock, London, 1987; *The Times*, 31 March 1987.
14 HFP, RH, unpublished autobiography, p.9.
15 *The Times*, 15 June 1984; RH, 'Modern medicine: prospects and problems'.
16 HFP, RH, 'Inequalities in health – a comment', 13 January 1983.
17 RH, 'Modern medicine: prospects and problems'.

Chapter 10: Medical ethics

1 RH, *Clinical Freedom*, The Rock Carling Fellowship, Nuffield Provincial Hospitals Trust, London, 1987, pp.37–8.

2 RH to LRH, 6 June 2003.

3 WCA, RH, 'Live and let die',Valedictory lecture delivered at Wolfson College, 10 June 1993.

4 Conference of Medical Royal Colleges and their Faculties in the United Kingdom, 'Diagnosis of brain death', *British Medical Journal*, 2, 1976, pp.1187–8; C. Pallis, 'Prognostic significance of a dead brain stem', *British Medical Journal*, 286, 8 January 1983, pp.123–4.

5 Conference of Medical Royal Colleges and their Faculties in the UK, *Report of a Working Party in Organ Transplantation in Neonates*, prepared for the Department of Health and Security, Crown Copyright, 1988.

6 M. Evans, 'Against brainstem death', in *Principles of Health Care Ethics* (ed. R. Gillon), John Wiley & Sons, Chichester, 1994, pp.1041–51.

7 C. Pallis, 'Prognostic significance of a dead brain stem', *British Medical Journal*, 286, 8 January 1983, pp.123–4.

8 S. J. Youngner, C. S. Landefeld, C. J. Coulton, B. W. Juknialis and M. Leary, ' "Brain death" and organ retrieval', *Journal of American Medical Association*, 261, 1989, pp.2205–10.

9 HFP, M. Lock, R. H. et al, 'Taking the brain out of death', draft ms; Z. Meradi.

10 WCA, RH, 'Live and let die', lecture 10 June 1993.

11 B. A. Brody, *Life and Decision Making*, Oxford University Press, Oxford, 1988.

12 Royal College of Physicians, *Resuscitation from Cardiopulmonary Arrest*, Report of a Working Party, Royal College of Physicians, London, 1987, p.7.

13 *RH, *Clinical Freedom*, p.72.

14 WCA, RH, 'Live and let die'.

15 B. R. Ferguson, 'Causing death or allowing to die. Developments in the law', *Journal of Medical Ethics*, 23, 1997, pp.368–372.

16 RH to LRH, 15 December 2003.

17 G. R. Dunstan, 'Conversations overheard', in *Consent in Medicine*, (eds) G. R. Dunstan and M. J. Seller, Oxford University Press, Oxford, 1983, pp.9–25; P. Baume, E. O'Malley and A. Bauman, 'Professed religious affiliation and the practice of euthanasia', *Journal of Medical Ethics*, 21, 1995, pp.49–54.

18 *The Independent* (London), 14 and 15 November 1991; HFP, RH to Cobden-Ramsay, 18 November 1991; Oswald Hickson Collier to Radcliffes, 5 December 1991.

19 Conference of Medical Royal Colleges and Their Faculties in the UK, *Report of the Working Party on the Supply of Donor Organs for Transplantation*, Prepared for the Department of Health and Social Security, Crown Copyright, 1987; *The Times*, London, 17 December 1986.

20 HFP, RH, December 1996.
21 I. Kennedy, R. A. Sells, A. S. Daar, R. D. Guttnam, RH, M. Lock, J. Radcliffe-Richards and N. Tilney, 'The case for "presumed consent" in organ donation', *The Lancet*, 351, 30 May 1998, pp.1650–2.
22 RH, 'Acquisition of kidneys for transplantation', in *Ethics and the Kidney*, (ed. N. G. Levinsky), Oxford University Press, Oxford, 2001, pp.130–143.
23 Australian and New Zealand Dialysis and Transplant Registry; HFP, RH, 'The case for transplantation with special reference to kidneys', June 1999.
24 RH, 'Acquisition of kidneys for transplantation', pp.131–4.
25 J. S. Cameron and RH, 'The ethics of organ transplantation reconsidered: Paid organ donation and the use of executed prisoners as donors', *Kidney International*, 55, 1999.
26 Royal College of Physicians, *Research on Healthy Volunteers*, Report of a Working Party, Royal College of Physicians, London, 1986.
27 RH, 'Acquisition of kidneys for transplantation', pp.139–142.
28 Ibid., pp.136–7.
29 RH, 'Commentary on "A bridge between hearts"', *Transplantation*, 76 (11), 15 December 2003.
30 HFP, 'Rethinking the "minority focus" in transplant research, I.F.T.E.'s guidelines for future research', IFTE, 11/7/2002.
31 HFP, IFTE, 'Presumed or informed consent: What do we know, what do we need to know', November 2002.
32 HFP, R. A. Sells, 'Some ethical issues in the allocation of kidneys'.
33 HFP, RH letter, 28 November 1969.
34 HFP, Strydom to Frederickson, 19 December 1969; Frederickson to Strydom, 26 February 1970.
35 HFP, Wyndham to Medawar, 22 December 1969; Brock to Hoffenberg, 19 May 1970.
36 HFP, Hoffenberg to Brock, undated; Brock to Hoffenberg, 20 June 1970; RH to LRH, 12 July 2004.
37 RH, 'Doctors under tension', *European Review*, 6 (2), 1998, pp.123–136.
38 RH, 'Medical involvement in torture', *Journal of Medical Ethics*, 19, 1993, pp.133–4.
39 L. Jacobsen and P. Vesti, *Torture Survivors – A New Group of Patients*, The Danish Nurses Association, Copenhagen, 1990.
40 RH to LRH, 17 March 2003.

Chapter 11: Medical activist
1   'Sir Raymond Hoffenberg', *Global Security*, 1992, p.2.
2   HFP, UKCCCR/20 February 1992.
3   *Sunday Times*, 27 May 1990; RH to LRH, 2 December 2003 and 28 May 2004.
4   RH to LRH, 12 August 2003.
5   *The Mental Health Foundation Spring Newsletter*, 1990; RH to LRH, 10 August 2003.

6 M.A. Lehmann to LRH, 24 May 2004; The Nuffield Provincial Hospitals Trust, Thirteenth Report 1991–1993, London, 1993 and Report and Accounts for the year ended 31 March 1994, p.1.

7 RH to LRH, 12 August 2003; *The Times*, 25 November 1991.

8 Wolfson Foundation Papers, RH to Lord Wolfson, 26 July 1991.

9 Victoria Harrison to LRH, 19 May 2004; RH, 'Health and Welfare', The Wolfson Foundation 7th Quinquennial Report 1986–1990, London, 1991, pp.4–7, and Triennial Report 1991–1993, pp.3–4.

10 RH to LRH, 27 August 2004.

11 N. Baldwin, *The Society for the Protection of Science and Learning Archive*, Bodleian Library, Oxford, 1988.

12 R.M. Cooper (ed.), *Refugee Scholars: Conversations with Tess Simpson*, Moorland Books, Leeds, 1992.

13 HFP, Esther Simpson to RH, 19 May 1993; A. Kenny to RH and others, 13 October 1992; Council for Assisting Refugee Academics, Minutes, 6 July 1999.

14 HFP, Zoe Landau to RH, 20 April 1999: Lord Wolfson to RH, 13 April 1999; Medical Foundation for the Care of Victims of Torture, Annual Review 1997.

15 RH, *Global Security*, Spring 1992, p.2.

16 UBA, Minutes of Faculty of Medicine and Dentistry, 24 January 1983.

17 'International physicians for the prevention of nuclear war', *The Lancet*, 25 June 1983, pp.1451–1452.

18 RH, L. Morrison and A. Haines, *The Times*, 11 November 1991.

19 RH, *Global Security*, Spring 1991, p.2.

Chapter 12: The later years

1 Derek Hoffenberg to LRH, 2 October 2005; Peter Hoffenberg to LRH, 20 January 2005.

2 M.A. Steinberg, C.M. Cartwright, J. Najman, S.M. MacDonald and G.Milliams, *Healthy Ageing Healthy Dying. Community and Health Professionals' Perspectives on End of Life Decision Making*, Department of Social and Preventive Medicine, University of Queensland, 1996.

3 M.A. Steinberg, C.M Cartwright, M.H. Parker and J.M. Najman, *Patient Self-Determination in Terminal Care, Phase 2*, Department of Social and Preventive Medicine, University of Queensland, 1997.

4 RH, 'Objections to assisted dying and my responses' in *House of Lords, Assisted Dying for the Terminally Ill (HL)*, 2004, Vol III, pp.45–47.

5 RH to LRH, 5 August 2005.

6 W. Beinart, *Twentieth-Century South Africa*, Oxford University Press, Oxford 2001, pp.272, 289, 291 and 317; RH to LRH, 16 December 2004.

7 P. Sidley, 'New health minister outlines future for South Africa', *British Medical Journal*, vol. 308, 1994, p.1525; RH to LRH, 16 December 2004; HFP, RH, 'Medical education in South Africa'.

8   RH, The *Times*, 15 February 1996.
9   RH to LRH, 16 December 2004 and 22 and 29 July 2005.
10 RH to LRH, 5 August 2005.
11 *Weekly Telegraph* (London), 19–25 May 2004; RH to *Weekly Telegraph* 25 May 2004.
12 Margaret Hoffenberg to LRH, 19 November 2004.

Summation

13 Hoffenberg, Sir Raymond (Bill), *Who's Who*, A.C. Black, London, 2003, p.1025.
14 Colleen Cartwright to LRH, 9 October 2005.

Index